A Companion to
The Current Justification Controversy

Books by John W. Robbins

Answer to Ayn Rand, 1974

The Case Against Indexation, 1976

The Case for Gold (author and editor), 1982

God's Hammer: The Bible and Its Critics (editor), 1982

Scripture Twisting in the Seminaries: Feminism, 1985

Cornelius Van Til: The Man and the Myth, 1986

Education, Christianity and the State (editor), 1987

Pat Robertson: A Warning to America, 1988

Gordon H. Clark: Personal Recollections
(author and editor), 1989

Essays on Ethics and Politics (editor), 1992

A Man of Principle: Essays in Honor of Hans F. Sennholz
(author and editor), 1992

Against the World: The Trinity Review 1978-1988
(author and editor), 1996

Without a Prayer: Ayn Rand and the Close of Her System, 1997

Ancient Philosophy (editor), 1997

Ecclesiastical Megalomania: The Economic and Political
Thought of the Roman Catholic Church, 1999

The Church Effeminate (author and editor), 2001

Against the Churches: The Trinity Review 1989-1998
(author and editor), 2002

Christ and Civilization, 2003

A Companion to The Current Justification Controversy
(author and editor), 2003

A Companion to
The Current Justification Controversy

John W. Robbins

The Trinity Foundation

Published by
The Trinity Foundation
Unicoi, Tennessee
http://www. trinityfoundation.org/
ISBN: 0-940931-64-8

Contents

The Roots and Fruits of the Shepherd Controversy

John W. Robbins

The Roots and Fruits of the Shepherd Controversy

John W. Robbins

THE GOSPEL of justification through belief alone is the central doctrine of Scripture, as Paul makes clear in his letter to the Romans.

After declaring this Gospel to be the power of God for salvation in *Romans* 1:16-17, the apostle discusses other doctrines and how they logically imply or are implied by the doctrine of justification through belief alone. In *Romans* 1:18 he immediately launches into a discussion of the sinfulness of men, their universal and total depravity, for the doctrine of total depravity is a necessary implication of the doctrine of justification through belief alone: No man can be justified by, through, or because of his own obedience or deeds, for if he could, justification would not be through belief alone. Every man, apart from the divine gift of imputed righteousness, which Paul will discuss at length beginning in chapter 3, is irremediably sinful and condemned by the perfect justice of God – the Jew first, as well as the Gentile. Therefore, all men's works – thoughts, words, and deeds – are sinful; and men are in need of a saviour, if they are to be saved at all. Paul strives to make the universal and total depravity of mankind clear, emphasizing that the Jews, who had great confidence in their circumcision, their lineage, and their *Torah*, were as guilty before God, and more so, than the uncircumcised Gentiles outside the law. The Jews too, if they are to be saved, must be justified through belief alone. Their "covenant faithfulness," their good works, as Paul says in *Philippians* 3, is rubbish, dung, excrement.

Christ made a similar point in telling Nicodemus, the teacher of the Jews, that he (and all Jews) must be born again before he could enter or see the kingdom of Heaven. Jesus preached the Gospel of justification through belief alone to Nicodemus: "And as Moses lifted up the serpent in the wilderness, even so must the Son of Man be lifted up, that whoever believes in him should not perish but have eternal life. For God so loved the world that he gave his only begotten Son, that whoever believes in him should not perish but have everlasting life. For God did not send his Son into the world to condemn the world, but that the world through him might be saved. He who believes in him is not condemned; but he who does not believe is condemned already, because he has not believed on the name of the only begotten Son of God" (*John* 3). Jesus had not come to rescue national Israel from Caesar, but the world from sin and death. And *whoever* – Jew or Gentile, Pharisee or Samaritan – did not believe the Gospel, was condemned already.

The Gospel of justification through belief alone was the central doctrine of the Christian Reformation in Europe in the sixteenth century. God planted that idea in the minds of Martin Luther, John Calvin, and thousands of others who turned the European world upside down by their preaching and writing. The super-spiritual, superstitious, and idolatrous rubbish of centuries (centuries that some men who claim to be Reformed call "Christian centuries") was swept into the trash bin of history by the Reformers, as the powerful Gospel of salvation through belief in Jesus Christ alone was widely proclaimed and believed. As a result of the Gospel of justification through belief alone, a new and unprecedented civilization arose in the West – a civilization that was relatively peaceful, humane, free, and prosperous.

Now, 500 years after the Reformation, most churches in the United States and Europe are once again apostate, having replaced the Gospel of Jesus Christ with the foolishness of religious fables and superstition, the rigmarole of religious ritual, scientific mythology, and a dozen other falsehoods. The current controversy over justification raging in American Reformed churches is a controversy only because a remnant still exists within those churches, a few Christians who understand and believe the Gospel of justification through belief alone. In most churches in the United States, there is no controversy over justification because no one in those churches understands or believes it. They have a theology of feeling and experience and social action, not a theology of understanding, truth, and Law and Gospel.

This writer first became aware of the controversy over justification more than twenty years ago, while he was working on Capitol Hill as an aide to a Member of Congress. One day, out of the blue, he received a call from Arthur Kuschke, a retired pastor in the Orthodox Presbyterian Church (OPC), seeking his help in the controversy concerning justification then raging in the Philadelphia Presbytery of the OPC and at Westminster Seminary. Mr. Kuschke and I had never met, though I had heard of him, but he had heard of me through the fledgling Trinity Foundation, which had just started publishing Dr. Gordon Clark's books. I was surprised to receive the call, for Mr. Kuschke had been one of the young men in

1944 who had followed the lead of the Faculty of Westminster Seminary in seeking to depose, without trial, Dr. Gordon H. Clark from the ministry. (The Faculty failed, but not before they had done irreparable damage to the OPC.) I asked Mr. Kuschke why he was calling me, and he surprised me again: In the current controversy over justification in the OPC and at Westminster Seminary, Mr. Kuschke had discovered that those who understood the doctrine of justification best, and were most stalwart in defending it, were students and sympathizers of Dr. Clark. He was calling to ask for help in defending the doctrine of justification against its opponents within the OPC and Westminster Seminary.

This time, nearly 40 years after the Clark-Van Til controversy in the 1940s, Mr. Kuschke was not on the side of the Westminster Faculty. John Murray and Cornelius Van Til had been among the most famous members of that Faculty, but Professor Murray had approved his successor, Norman Shepherd, and Professor Van Til was defending Mr. Shepherd's Neolegalism. To his great credit, Arthur Kuschke directly opposed Shepherd, and indirectly opposed his famous teachers at Westminster Seminary. Mr. Kuschke continues, despite his advanced years, to oppose this heresy in the OPC, of which I shall say more later.

When Norman Shepherd was finally dismissed from the Faculty of Westminster Seminary in early 1982, I, like many others, I suppose, thought the Seminary had solved the immediate problem by removing a false teacher. I was wrong. As Dr. Mark Karlberg explained in another of our publications, *The Changing of the Guard*, the Seminary had removed one teacher (Shepherd) from its Faculty, but had allowed his false teaching to continue at the Seminary. For the past twenty years, though

Norman Shepherd has not been on the Faculty of Westminster Seminary, men who defended him and agreed with him in these matters have been teaching there, inculcating their views of election, justification, and covenant in hundreds of men who are now pastors, missionaries, and teachers in Presbyterian and Reformed churches, schools, and seminaries. So, when Presbyterian and Reformed Publishing Company (which has had close ties to the Faculty of Westminster Seminary for at least three decades) published Norman Shepherd's book *The Call of Grace* in late 2000, there were plenty of defenders of his erroneous views ensconced in the churches, and they responded to his call by vigorously defending the errors they had learned. The result has been a widespread outbreak of opposition to the Gospel of justification through belief alone in the very churches that profess to be Reformed.

The first justification controversy from 1975 to 1982 was never properly settled. The Orthodox Presbyterian Church transferred Norman Shepherd in good standing to the Christian Reformed Church, where he pastored churches for almost two more decades. Westminster Seminary released him from its Faculty, apparently because of pressure from some alumni, not because a majority of the Faculty or the administration thought he was teaching heresy. In fact, a majority of the Faculty of the Seminary defended Shepherd and his views, and to this day they continue to do so.

Now, more than twenty years later, the controversy has erupted again, but this time it has not been centralized in one Seminary or one Presbytery. The disciples of Shepherd and his friends are spread throughout the churches, ensconced as pastors, teachers, and ruling Elders. As a result, church courts in three denominations – the Presbyterian Church in America, the Reformed Presbyterian Church in the United States, and the Orthodox Presbyterian Church – have denounced Shepherd's views as heretical or taken action against men influenced by Shepherd who were promoting views of salvation contrary to Scripture and the *Westminster Confession.* These judicial actions have not stemmed the tide of apostasy in Reformed circles. Rather, they have disclosed how serious and widespread the departure from the Gospel is. The cancer of Neolegalism was not killed in 1982, and it has now metastasized throughout Reformed and Presbyterian churches in America. The Philadelphia Presbytery of the OPC, by failing to take proper disciplinary action against Shepherd, his supporters, and their views when it had the opportunity to do so more than twenty years ago, has permitted the leaven of the Pharisees to leaven the whole lump.

Sympathizers and opponents of Norman Shepherd can agree on one thing: Neither the Presbytery of Philadelphia nor Westminster Seminary treated Norman Shepherd justly. And there their agreement ends. His supporters think he was treated unfairly and should never have been questioned for his views on justification, let alone removed from the Faculty. His opponents think his supporters in both the Presbytery and the Seminary managed to shortcircuit the proceedings in both Presbytery and Seminary, which allowed him and his false teaching to escape clear condemnation. John Frame, a member of the Westminster Faculty at the time of the controversy, later pointed out the unfairness of dismissing Shepherd for teaching doctrines that were being taught by other members of the Faculty as well. And Frame was right. But the injustice lay not in dismissing Shepherd, as Frame imagined, but in allowing other Faculty members to remain at Westminster.

Norman Shepherd taught at Westminster Seminary for 18 years, the last seven of which were awash in the controversy he had caused by teaching doctrines contrary to Scripture and the *Westminster Confession of Faith*. During those years he taught hundreds of future pastors, missionaries, and teachers false doctrine about the covenant of grace, election, faith, the sacraments, and justification. When he was finally removed from the Faculty of the Seminary, and the Shepherd controversy seemed to end, he departed in good standing from the Orthodox Presbyterian Church and Westminster Seminary to the Christian Reformed Church. There he pastored two congregations for another 18 years, and retired.

But while the controversy subsided, and Shepherd himself departed, his teaching remained. His doctrines continued to be taught at Westminster Seminary by men who had defended him during the controversy: Samuel T. Logan, Jr., now President of the Seminary; Richard B. Gaffin, Jr., now senior member of the Faculty; and John M. Frame, who left the Philadelphia campus and taught at Westminster West in California before moving on to Reformed Theological Seminary, to name three.

Their teaching, and Shepherd's own teaching in the Christian Reformed Church, ensured that in 1999 he would be invited to deliver the Robinson Lectures at Erskine Theological Seminary in North Carolina, and in 2000 publish a new book, *The Call of Grace*, which included a paper he had written in 1975. In 25 years he had not corrected his views. What had changed was the number of people who now agreed with him.

Who would have thought, in 1975 when the controversy began, that within 25 years Biblical Christianity would have been replaced by a clever counterfeit in many American Presbyterian and Reformed churches? Who would have dreamt that in The Year of Our Lord 2003 the major theological battle-front in Reformed churches would be the Gospel of Jesus Christ – the doctrine of justification by faith alone? Yet that is exactly what has happened.

The Neolegalist flood now surging through churches and schools has several sources. In Reformed churches, as we have seen in Dr. Robertson's history of the Shepherd controversy, this Neolegalism claims to be covenantal and Reformed, even Calvinist. It has already swept some seminary graduates back to Rome – Scott Hahn (Gordon-Conwell Seminary) and Robert Sungenis (Westminster Seminary) are two of the more famous – and it is being propagated by teachers and preachers who apparently do not have the courage (and perhaps not even the integrity) of Hahn or Sungenis, and so do not intend to leave their positions of income and influence in Reformed churches and schools. To all appearances, these proponents of covenantal Neolegalism intend to stay in Protestant institutions and, in effect, transform them into theological colonies of Rome.

Of course they deny that they are doing any such thing, and assert they are rediscovering a "rich tradition" that the "modern" interpretation of the Reformation has obscured. One of the tactics of these theological revisionists is to reinterpret the Reformers, so that they said something different from the Romanists, but not much different. We modern Presbyterians, the Neolegalists tell us, have misunderstood the Reformers, who had a medieval mindset, and we misunderstand the Apostle Paul himself, who had a Jewish mindset. Specifically on the matter of justification, they confidently assert, neither Paul nor Calvin was a Lutheran.

In Presbyterian circles this movement is associated with names (in addition to those already mentioned) such as Dr. Peter Leithart (Presbyterian Church in America, New St. Andrews College, Idaho), Dr. Peter Lillback (Presbyterian Church in America, Reformed Episcopal Seminary), Andrew Sandlin (Center for Cultural Leadership), Steven Schlissel (Messiah's Congregation, New York), Steven Wilkins (Presbyterian Church in America, Auburn Avenue Pastors Conference), Mark Horne (Presbyterian Church in America), John Kinnaird (Orthodox Presbyterian Church), Joseph Braswell (Reconstructionist writer), Dr. Greg Bahnsen (chief theologian of the Theonomy movement), Dr. Gary North (prolific author and chief theoretician in the Reconstructionist/Theonomy movement), and James Jordan (author in the Reconstructionist/Theonomy movement). In other circles, such names as Daniel Fuller, John Armstrong, and Douglas Wilson are prominent in the movement away from the Gospel and Christ.

Although the streams of thought that have contributed to the flood of Neolegalism surging through the churches differ from each other, and some might even criticize some others, they all flow into the same soteriological river that is sweeping the churches away. What unites them is their opposition to the proposition that the justification of sinners is through faith alone. Some of them deny it frankly and candidly. Others affirm it, as Norman Shepherd did all through the Shepherd controversy, while asserting and defending contrary views as well. Others redefine the principal terms so that they can equivocally affirm justification by faith alone.

There are, however, some salient and false doctrines of these schools of thought that they hold more or less in common:

1. They deny or diminish individual election to salvation;

2. They condemn individualism;

3. They deny that faith is assent to understood propositions, and belittle or deny propositional and literal truth;

4. They deny or equivocally affirm that faith alone justifies;

5. They deny that knowledge is necessary for salvation, and condemn those who insist on knowledge and understanding as "gnostics";

6. They deny the covenant of works;

7. They deny or diminish the meritorious work of Christ as the representative of and substitute for his people;

8. They deny or diminish the imputation of the active righteousness of Christ to believers;

9. They assert that ritual baptism regenerates, washes away sins, and is necessary for salvation;

10. They assert that the "covenantally elect," which is the only election human beings can know, can lose their justification and salvation;

11. They assert that the "final justification" of believers depends on their lifelong performance;

12. They assert that God accepts less than perfect obedience for fulfilling the conditions of salvation;

13. They assert that persons who are unbelievers and reprobate are nevertheless "members of the covenant";

14. They assert that good works are necessary to obtain or retain salvation;

15. They assert that "Biblical theology" is superior to systematic theology;

16. They assert that ecclesiology is soteriology.

17. They deny the Biblical contrast between Law and Gospel.

Because the various Neolegalists are still working out the implications of their assumptions (1) not all Neolegalists have arrived at all these conclusions; (2) they disagree with each other on details; and (3) more conclusions are still being developed. This is very much a *move*ment, but it is clearly a movement away from the Gospel of Jesus Christ to some form of covenantal nomism, in which one's final salvation depends (at least in part) on one's performance.

Let us look briefly at a few of the theological streams contributing to the flood of Neolegalism.

Neo-orthodoxy. The Neo-orthodox theology of Karl Barth, a sort of counterfeit Calvinism, included the notion that there is only one covenant – a covenant of grace – between God and men. There is such a great gulf fixed between the Creator and the creature that any covenant the Creator might make with his creatures must be a covenant of grace, and cannot be a covenant of justice, works, or merit. Even in the Garden, before the fall of Adam, God came in grace to Adam. There was no covenant of works, no principle of merit or justice by which righteous Adam, by his obedience, could have earned the favor of God and everlasting life. Barth's mono-covenantalism has been widely accepted in Reformed circles, together with his infinite Creator-creature dichotomy. Barth's view, is, of course, not the view of the Reformers, and not what the Bible says. But because his theology sounded like a "theology of grace" as well as a "theology of paradox," it was widely accepted in Reformed circles.

Roman Catholicism. A second stream in the flood of Neolegalism is the theology of Roman Catholicism. In *The Call of Grace* Shepherd expresses his desire to furnish the theology that will unite Protestants and Roman Catholics. It is Catholicism, rather than Protestantism, in his view, that correctly understands the letter of *James*. He writes: "What is required from Rome [and from Protestants as well] is a change from a works/merit paradigm for understanding the way of salvation to a covenantal paradigm.... This change in paradigm would provide a proper basis for Rome's legitimate insistence that full credence be given to *James* 2:24, *Galatians* 5:6, and similar passages" (*The Call of Grace*, 61). Shepherd here tips his hand, for he thinks that it is Rome, not the Reformers, that gives "full credence" to *James*. And it is Rome, not the Reformers, that "legitimately insists" on this "full credence."

Shepherd rejects the "Lutheran" (Calvin was a Lutheran in this sense) Law/Gospel distinction, and favors a Romish view that mingles Law and Gospel together in the way of salvation. The result is a soteriology that in principle is Roman Catholic. For both Shepherd and Rome, qualifying for Heaven is a lifelong process. That process begins, not with faith, but with the visible sign of the covenant, ritual baptism, which, in Shepherd's words, "marks the point...of conversion." The baptized person, who is "covenantally elect" by virtue of his baptism, and the recipient of saving grace, is required to obey in order to retain his status in the covenant and receive "final salvation." Shepherd, like Rome, appeals to *Matthew* 7:21-23 as proving his point that only those who do good works will enter Heaven.[1] The works that the baptized person does are, of course, done by the grace of God, which is why both Rome and Shepherd say they believe in salvation by grace.

---

1. For a refutation of this view, see John W. Robbins, "Justification and Judgment," *The Trinity Review*, November/December 2001.

The New Perspective on Paul. A third stream of thought contributing to the flood of Neolegalism and to the widespread defection from the Gospel in conservative churches at the end of the twentieth century and at the beginning of the twenty-first is the so-called New Perspective on Paul. After the Shepherd controversy began, this movement, also influenced by Barth, swept through academia and became the majority report among New Testament academics. The New Perspective is usually traced to the publication of E. P. Sanders' book *Paul and Palestinian Judaism* in 1977. This movement argued, among other things, that the Reformers, especially Luther, misunderstood first century Judaism, for it was not a works-religion. If it was not a works-religion, then Paul's doctrine and polemic of justification cannot be aimed at legalism, but at the ethnic and national "boundary markers" – food laws and circumcision, for example – that separated Jews from Gentiles. Justification is the ecumenical doctrine that explains how Gentiles are made part of the covenant people without adopting the boundary markers of the Jews. Justification is a sociological doctrine, rather than a "scheme of soteriology." This argument has been widely accepted, and in some putatively Reformed churches, the opinions of one of its major proponents, N. T. Wright, Anglican Bishop of Durham, have been welcomed. Dr. Robert Reymond discusses the New Perspective in his essay below.

Reconstructionism. Beginning in earnest in the 1980s, with a flood of books and an apparently bottomless well of cash, the Christian Reconstruction movement began setting forth its program for the conquest and dominion of the world. Led by men such as Rousas Rushdoony, his son-in-law Gary North, and Greg Bahnsen, the movement promoted the views of Shepherd as part of its program for social action, publishing Shepherd himself in *The Journal of Christian Reconstruction* in the 1970s, while the Shepherd controversy was raging.[2]

Randy Booth writes:

> ...in the early 1990s, ten years after Shepherd's leaving Westminster Seminary, he [Rousas Rushdoony] did not hesitate to publish an *explicit* defense of Shepherd's views. This apologetic for Shepherd is found in Joseph Braswell's essay, "Lord of Life: The Confession of Lordship and Saving Faith" [*Journal of Christian Reconstruction*, Volume 13, Number 1, 1990-1991, Gary Moes, editor].

In 1991 a former Westminster Seminary student (though not a graduate), Dr. Gary North, an economic historian, published a book (*Westminster's Confession*) dedicated to Norman Shepherd, "the most accomplished instructor I had at Westminster Seminary, who combined Machen's eschatological optimism, Van Til's presuppositional apologetic, and Murray's precise theological language. He was a loyal defender of Westminster's [Seminary's] original confession." Shepherd the noble Reformed scion and martyr is a figment of North's imagination, but North has spent millions of dollars promoting Shepherd's views and his own doctrinal novelties.[3] "When

---

2. "In the midst of the Shepherd controversy at Westminster Seminary in the mid and late 70s, Rushdoony published Norman Shepherd in the *Journal of Christian Reconstruction* [Volume 3, Number 2, 1976-1977, Gary North, editor]." Randy Booth, "Caution and Respect in Controversy," 9.

3. North writes, "...since 1981, when I finally got control over enough money to put the theonomic publication machine into high gear. You can put out a lot of books by spending a million or so dollars, net, not counting any of the income from book sales" (3). North made millions scaring people

Shepherd was fired," North thundered, "every Faculty member should have quit in protest" (xxi). One must agree with North that every Faculty member who agreed with Shepherd should have resigned, if not in protest, then in integrity. But they did not. They continued to occupy their positions of influence and income in order to continue to advance views that had disrupted the peace and purity of the Seminary for seven years.

North denied that there was any theological reason for Shepherd's firing: "In 1982 the Board failed to renew Norman Shepherd's contract. (Try and find anyone who can tell you what theological grounds they had. His presbytery found none") (42-43). Despite the fact that his Ph.D. is in history, North is not a reliable historian. When he wrote this line, Palmer Robertson's monograph *The Current Justification Controversy* had been written and distributed in manuscript form for eight years. North did not have to look far for someone to tell him the theological reasons for Shepherd's dismissal. But he missed them.

Actually, North did not need to read even Dr. Robertson's monograph. He might have read the rather mildly and discreetly worded "Reason and Specifications Supporting the Action of the Board of Trustees in Removing Professor Shepherd, Approved by the Executive Committee of the Board (Feb-

---

to death about imminent hyperinflation, permanent price controls, AIDS pandemics, imminent nuclear war, and most notorious of all, the worldwide computer catastrophe caused by Y2K, which North gleefully anticipated. Some people love to be scared (they go to horror movies, too), and North has profited handsomely from their weakness. He has funded the publication of perhaps 200 books, most of which would never have seen the light of day without his massive subsidies.

ruary 26, 1982)." There he would have found the following theological reasons for Shepherd's dismissal stated:

> In spite of modifications that Mr. Shepherd has made in his expressions, the Board finds that the problems in his teaching are not resolved, and that they are inherent in his view of the "covenant dynamic." Although Mr. Shepherd appeals to the history of Reformed covenantal theology to support his position, the Board finds that Mr. Shepherd's construction is distinctive. It is in the distinctive elements and emphases of his theology of the covenant that the problem appears.
>
> In his "covenant dynamic" Mr. Shepherd develops a formula that permits him to join good works to faith as the characteristic and qualifying response to grace. Obedience is the proper, full, and comprehensive term for all covenantal response, and specifically for our response in the covenant of grace.
>
> The "covenant dynamic" of Mr. Shepherd makes the function of our obedience in the covenant to be the same as the function of the obedience of Adam in the covenant before the fall ("Life in Covenant with God," Tapes 1, 2). Mr. Shepherd finds one covenantal pattern in all of Scripture. The pattern joins God's free grace and our response in faithful obedience.
>
> The omission of any clear treatment of Christ as the covenant Head, of his active obedience, of the imputation of his righteousness in the fulfillment of the covenant command, of his probation in our place (this in a treatment of the covenant that professes to be distinctively Reformed, after years of discussion) evidences a lack of clarity that cannot but cause concern.
>
> Mr. Shepherd insists that the threat of the curse is a necessary part of the covenant structure for Adam, for Israel, and for us. It promises blessing for the faithful

24

and curse for the unfaithful. He has described the reservation that the threat of eternal death does not apply to believers as a "moral influence" theory of the warnings of Scripture (Faculty conference, October 26, 1981). He urged before the Board that just as Adam's posterity would not be "off the hook" if Adam had obeyed, but would be bound to fulfill the condition of obedience, so the posterity of Christ are not "off the hook."

By rejecting the distinction between the covenant of works and the covenant of grace as defined in the Westminster Standards, and by failing to take account in the structure of the "covenantal dynamic" of Christ's fulfillment of the covenant by his active obedience as well as by his satisfaction of its curse, Mr. Shepherd develops a uniform concept of covenantal faithfulness for Adam, for Israel, and for the New Covenant people. The danger is that both the distinctiveness of the covenant of grace and of the new covenant fullness of the covenant of grace will be lost from view and that obedience as the way of salvation will swallow up the distinct and primary function of faith.[4]

North himself tells us why he missed all this: Like many of his books, *Westminster's Confession* is a "quickie." His model as an author is Isaac Asimov, who cranked out hundreds of books during his lifetime, and North long ago determined to do the same. This emphasis on quantity of production fitted his strategy for winning debates perfectly. He explained – more accurately, he boasted of – his strategy in *Westminster's Confession*:

> When in the late 1970's, I decided that if I ever had enough money in the ICE [Institute for Christian Economics] bank account to run my own version of the tar

4. See below for the full text of *Reason and Specifications*.

baby strategy, I would launch it. But in my version I am a chatty tar baby, and the seminaries are silent rabbits. I keep saying in print that they do not have the theological goods to deal with the crises of modern society because they neglect biblical law and postmillennialism, and they just sit there, silent, proving my point. Finally, one of the Faculty members hits back, and from that point on, he is trapped. I finance a book in reply. The only way for him to save face publicly is to write a reply, and then I publish another book. This goes on until there are no more replies. Then I announce a victory and target a new victim. This strategy is expensive, but it works [3-4].

One book that North would love to publish is Professor Richard B. Gaffin, Jr.'s history of the Shepherd controversy: "I will say this for Gaffin: he tried to defend Shepherd. After Gaffin retires (or Westminster East goes bankrupt), perhaps he will write a book about the whole ugly affair. If I am still around, I will publish it" (224-225).

Although not a Reconstructionist, Professor Gaffin has been, in the words of Dr. Mark Karlberg, "Shepherd's ardent defender and the co-father of the new, anti-Reformational teaching at Westminster Seminary."[5] Karlberg elaborates:

> Gaffin and Shepherd are convinced that the Protestant/Reformed tradition is in need of correction and modification in its understanding of the Biblical doctrine of justification by faith. At no point in the [Shepherd] controversy, from the beginning to the present, has Gaffin taken exception to Shepherd's formulations. He has vigorously defended Shepherd thesis by thesis,

5. *The Changing of the Guard.* The Trinity Foundation, 2001, 28.

point by point, adamantly insisting upon the soundness of Shepherd's views [30].

Professor Gaffin, who remains the most dominant member of the Faculty, and the current President, Samuel Logan, have succeeded in removing all opposition from within the Philadelphia Faculty, even though the Seminary denies barring Shepherd's critics from Faculty appointments.... The pernicious, insidious teaching of the Shepherd school is now entrenched in the Seminary and in the churches it serves. From all appearances, there is little hope of seeing a return of Westminster to its original position and role in the propagation and defense of historic Calvinism [37- 38].

Still another Reconstructionist is Greg Bahnsen. Randy Booth quotes Bahnsen's view of justification as follows:

...some people will say James can't mean the word justify in a forensic sense, because then he would contradict Paul. Paul says we are justified by faith, not works. James says we are justified by works. So if they both mean "justify" in the forensic sense, there is a contradiction. Well, I don't think so, because in *Galatians* 5:6 Paul teaches exactly what James does. Paul says we are justified by faith working by love. We are justified by working, active, living faith. I think that's what James is teaching. They mean exactly the same thing. But nevertheless some people have insisted – and this has been a bone of controversy in my own denomination [the OPC] even, because a professor at Westminster Seminary insisted James means this in the forensic sense.

Now...people who don't like that say, It is to be taken in the demonstrative sense. The problem is, the demonstrative sense of the word justify means "to show some-

one to be righteous," and that doesn't relieve the contradiction between James and Paul, because Paul in *Romans* 4 looks at Abraham as an example of how God
justifies the ungodly. James is saying, Look at how God
justifies someone demonstrated as godly. The contradiction is not relieved. And so what you really get – and
this is crucial, this is a crucial point – modern interpreters who don't like what I am suggesting and what Professor Shepherd is suggesting end up saying that to justify in *James* 2 really means "to demonstrate justification...."

...the reason Paul and James are not contrary to one
another is because the only kind of faith that will justify
us is working faith, and the only kind of justification
ever presented in the Bible after the fall is a justification
by working faith, a faith that receives its merit from God
and proceeds to work as a regenerated, new person.[6]

Like his mentor Van Til, whom we will discuss in a moment, Bahnsen explicitly defended Shepherd and his views on
justification:

But then again John Murray retires at Westminster
and you have a man [Shepherd] who was very competent who took his place and because he was so competent and wrote in a way that didn't favor mass, well, the
opinion of many in positions of influence, he was
moved out of his position.[7]

Booth points out that "Instead of condemning Shepherd as
dangerous, erroneous or heretical, Bahnsen sees his dismissal
from Westminster Theological Seminary as the loss of a 'very

6. Greg L. Bahnsen, audio tape lecture #GB449b, 1986.
7. Greg L. Bahnsen, audio tape lecture #GB178, 1986.

competent' man." [8] Booth quotes a letter from Roger Wagner, a minister in the Orthodox Presbyterian Church and Bahnsen's best friend:

> Greg and I both had Shepherd for the Doctrine of the Holy Spirit in seminary and were very, very appreciative of his teaching (as well as his preaching in chapel and elsewhere from time to time). His work on the covenant and justification were [sic] not as developed (or public) at that time, but in later years (after the controversy erupted) when Greg and I talked about "Shepherd's position" on these matters, he was always very favorable to Shepherd's concerns and formulations....
>
> He thought, as do I, that Shepherd's critics either don't understand Shepherd's covenantal interests and concerns or don't want to (as is often the case with the critics of Van Til and Bahnsen as well). I'm not sure if it was Shepherd who pointed us to [Daniel] Fuller's book on law and gospel, but Greg also appreciated that discussion because it wrestles in a more sophisticated way with the question of the relation between redemption and ethics in the covenant (old and new). I think you said (somewhere) that Greg told you he agreed with Fuller's interpretation of some texts over his own after reading Fuller's book....
>
> I'm absolutely sure if Greg were still with us, he'd be squarely on the "Shepherd side" of this issue....
>
> I think the covenant theology formulated by [Norman] Shepherd, [Steven] Schlissel, [N.T.] Wright, and others is not only biblical, but also our strongest bastion against the growing "Lutheranism" and antinomianism in Reformed circles. [9]

8. Booth, "Caution and Respect in Controversy," 13.
9. Booth, "Caution and Respect in Controversy," 13-14.

In addition to his best friend, his son, David Bahnsen, also has claimed that "my father...publicly and privately embraced [Shepherd's] views. Even apart from his personal comments to me throughout my life about Professor Shepherd being one of his all-time favorite seminary instructors...."[10]

Biblical Theology. Still another stream contributing to the flood of Neolegalism is the "Biblical theology" of Daniel Fuller, Professor at Fuller Theological Seminary in California. Two of his two books, *Gospel and Law: Contrast or Continuum?* and *The Unity of the Bible: Unfolding God's Plan for Humanity,* have deeply influenced many, including his devoted student and bestselling author John Piper. Fuller specially thanks Piper for his editorial and theological help in producing *The Unity of the Bible,* and Piper acknowledges his profound debt to Fuller in his own book, *Future Grace.*

The unity of mind between Piper and Fuller is reflected in these statements:

> And very special thanks are due to John Piper, senior pastor at Bethlehem Baptist Church of Minneapolis, who in the midst of his many pastoral responsibilities took three full days to scrutinize an early draft of the first twelve chapters. He gave another six days of a sabbatical in the summer of 1990 to taping numerous queries concerning the basic outline of the manuscript. He also gave several days of his 1991 vacation to making queries of the final draft of the manuscript. These efforts helped me correct and clarify a number of important matters. His writing of the Foreword reflects his deep investment in this work.[11]

10. Booth, "Caution and Respect in Controversy," 14.
11. Daniel Fuller, "Acknowledgments," *The Unity of the Bible,* viii.

No book besides the Bible has had a greater influence on my life than Daniel Fuller's *The Unity of the Bible*. When I first read it as a classroom syllabus over twenty years ago, everything began to change.

The hallowing of God's name (*Matthew* 6:9) flamed up as the center of my prayers. God's passion for his glory (*Isaiah* 48:9-11) stopped seeming selfish and became the very fountain of grace that flings all wonders of love into his being. God's law stopped being at odds with the gospel. It stopped being a job description for earning wages under a so-called covenant of works (which I never could find in the Bible) and became a precious doctor's prescription that flows from faith in the divine Physician (*Romans* 9:32)....

The life-changing effects of Fuller's *The Unity of the Bible* are not a fluke....

Over 100 people at our church have worked their way through *The Unity of the Bible* in pastor-led small group settings. The vision of God and his purposes in this book is the theological backbone of our life together. And, perhaps most important of all, the great global plan of God unfolded in this book has become the flame that drives the missionary engine of our church.[12]

Daniel Fuller's vision of the Christian life as an "obedience of faith" is the garden in which the plants of my ponderings have grown. Almost three decades of dialogue on the issues in this book have left a deep imprint. If I tried to show it with footnotes, they would be on almost every page. His major work, *The Unity of the Bible* (Zondervan Publishing House, 1992), is explanatory background to most of what I write.[13]

12. John Piper, "Foreword," *The Unity of the Bible*, x-xii.
13. John Piper, "Preface," *Future Grace*, 7.

Nothing I have said here diminishes the burden of this book to press home vigorously the future-oriented aspect of faith. I stand shoulder to shoulder with Daniel Fuller and the conviction of his book, *Unity of the Bible*, that "a faith that only looks back to Christ's death and resurrection is not sufficient.... Forgiveness for the Christian also depends on having, like Abraham, a futuristic faith in God's promises. Thus we cannot regard justifying faith as sufficient if it honors only the past fact of Christ's death and resurrection but does not honor the future promises of God, thus mocking his character and integrity."[14]

Like Barth, Fuller denies that Scripture teaches a covenant of works in which God promised everlasting life to Adam on the condition of his perfect, personal obedience; and threatened everlasting death if Adam failed to meet that condition. One consequence of this denial of the covenant of works is that if Adam was not a party to the covenant of works, as these men assert, then neither was Christ, the Second and Last Adam. Therefore, Christ could not, did not, and was not supposed to pay the just debts of, and earn salvation for, his people. As the Second and Last Adam, Christ did not by his active and passive obedience perfectly fulfill the Law of God, pay the just and legal debts of his people, and merit their salvation. Merit and justice are categories eliminated by this mono-covenantalism.

Thus the denial of the covenant of works is a direct attack on the justice of God, on the imputation of Adam's sin to his children, on the active obedience and work of Christ, and on

14. *Future Grace*, 206-207.

the imputation of Christ's active obedience and righteousness to believers. By denying that Adam and Christ, as federal heads of their respective races, were under a covenant of works, each Adam being required to fulfill the terms of the covenant, one failing miserably, and the other succeeding perfectly, the Neolegalists put all believers on probation, and make their salvation depend on their personal obedience. They explicitly deny the covenant of works for Adam and Christ, and implicitly assert that each sinner must work his way to Heaven – with God's help and grace, of course. (In this they do not differ from Rome.) By denying, ignoring, or depreciating the decisive and final work of Christ the Mediator two thousand years ago, they make each sinner fulfill at least some of the conditions of his own salvation.

Fuller characterizes the justice principle that informs the covenant of works as "the highest kind of blasphemy." "Were...covenant theolog[ians] to perceive that the obedience of faith is the only kind of obedience that is ever acceptable to the 'God who will not give his glory to another' (Isa 42:8), they could make the blessing Adam was to receive after passing his probationary test a work of grace rather than the payment of debt, and therefore would not make themselves vulnerable to the charge that the kind of righteousness Adam and Christ were to perform was the highest kind of blasphemy."[15]

---

15. Daniel P. Fuller, "A Response on the Subject of Works and Grace," *Presbyterion: A Journal for the Eldership*, Spring-Fall 1983, 76. *Presbyterion* is, of course, the theological journal of Covenant Theological Seminary, which refused to publish Palmer Robertson's *The Current Justification Controversy*.

Fuller believes the covenant of works involves the " highest kind of blasphemy" because it implies that man can, by obeying God, "put God in his debt." By using a speculative notion of God's dealings with man, rather than the actual covenantal arrangements revealed in Scripture in which God commits himself to punish and reward the disobedience and obedience of the First and Last Adams as the federal representatives of their races, Fuller eliminates the Bible's doctrine of salvation. There can be no salvation unless God is just. *Justification is about justice.* (See *Romans* 3:21-26.) It is appalling that so-called Christian theologians do not – cannot – understand that elementary point. Divine justice logically entails merit and demerit, desert, reward and punishment. Annihilate God's justice, and all that remains is not grace or mercy, as these Neolegalists think, but caprice, whimsy, and uncertainty. Divine grace and mercy have meaning only within the framework of divine justice. Remove justice, and all that remains is injustice, not mercy.

By eliminating the antithesis between Law and Gospel, Fuller eliminates the Gospel:

> I then had to accept the very drastic conclusion that the antithesis between law and Gospel established by Luther, Calvin, and the covenant theologians could no longer stand up under the scrutiny of Biblical theology.[16]

> I would say that Moses was justified by the work, or obedience, of faith.... [There are] many passages in Scripture in which good works are made the instrumental cause of justification.[17]

16. Daniel P. Fuller, *Gospel and Law*, xi.
17. Daniel P. Fuller, "A Response on the Subject of Works and Grace," *Presbyterion*, 1983, 79.

Calvin, according to Fuller, had to go through exegetical and logical "contortions" and to "fly in the face of Scripture's plain language" in order to maintain the Reformation doctrine of justification by faith alone.[18] Fuller's arguments have been widely adopted by pastors and teachers in Reformed churches and schools. Sympathizers with Shepherd have seen in Fuller more support for their covenantal Neolegalism.

Gaffin and Bavinck. As Palmer Robertson noted in *The Current Justification Controversy*, the Faculty of Westminster Seminary reacted angrily to the May 4, 1981 open letter signed by 45 theologians.[19] One member of the Faculty, Professor Richard B. Gaffin, Jr., wrote a seven-page response addressed to "those concerned for the ministry of Westminster Seminary."

In his May 19, 1981 letter, Mr. Gaffin first raised the usual procedural objection: "Is this communication [the May 4 letter] the constructive or even proper way to prosecute concerns about doctrinal error? Does it really serve the well-being of the church to widely publicize loosely supported allegations of serious doctrinal error?... One thing is certain: the effect of this communication has been to undermine, without due process, what is most precious to Mr. Shepherd as a seminary professor, the confidence in him of the churches he is seeking to serve."

Now of course, confidence in Norman Shepherd had been undermined six years earlier, when his students, examined by presbyteries for ordination, had confessed that justification is

18. Daniel P. Fuller, "A Response on the Subject of Works and Grace," *Presbyterion*, 1983, 79.
19. For the full text of this "Letter of Concern," see below.

by faith and works. Confidence in Professor Shepherd was not first undermined by a letter sent in 1981, but by Professor Shepherd's faithful students in 1974 and 1975. That loss of confidence beginning in 1974 and 1975 marks the beginning of the controversy.

Furthermore, charges had been filed against Shepherd in the Presbytery of Philadelphia in 1977, four years before Gaffin alleges that there was a lack of due process in this case. Moreover, as Robertson's history shows, the Seminary Faculty, Board, and administration had been engaged in discussions and conferences with Shepherd for six years prior to Gaffin's sending his May 19 letter. Professor Gaffin knew all this when he wrote, "without due process."

Dr. Robertson's history also shows that the allegations against Shepherd were not "loosely supported." There was ample documentation of his views in audiotapes of his classroom lectures, various papers he had written for the Faculty and Board of the Seminary, and essays that he had published. What apparently made the May 4, 1981 letter so disturbing to the Westminster Faculty was the fact that it informed the larger church – not just the Seminary community, which had for years succeeded in keeping the controversy largely contained within its walls – of serious doctrinal problems in the teaching at Westminster Seminary.

The bulk of Gaffin's letter, after he raises the procedural objections, is a labored attempt to ferret out theological precedent for Shepherd's erroneous views on justification in Herman Bavinck (Gaffin includes a page of newly translated material from Bavinck's *Gereformeerde Dogmatiek* with his letter), in the *Westminster Confession of Faith*, and even in John Calvin.

With regard to Calvin, Mr. Gaffin spends more than a page discussing a single paragraph from Calvin's commentary on *Ezekiel*. This is a pattern that Peter Lillback, who received his Th.D. from Westminster Seminary in 1985 for his dissertation, *The Binding of God*, also used in his attempt to transform Calvin into a teacher of justification by faith and works.[20] And Samuel T. Logan, Jr., a member of the Faculty since 1979, and a defender of Shepherd who became president of the Seminary in 1991, published an essay in *The Westminster Theological Journal* in 1984 maintaining that Jonathan Edwards held a similar view of justification.[21] Dr. Logan concluded: "Edwards believes that full justice must be done to Biblical passages such as this [*Matthew* 25:31-46] and he correctly does that justice in identifying feeding the hungry and visiting the sick and clothing the naked as *conditions* of justification. With obedience such as this, justification shall be and without it justification shall not be" (45, emphasis in the original).

From the 1980s on, these revisionist efforts by Shepherd sympathizers received a boost from the growing influence of the so-called New Perspective on Paul. According to this new school of thought, dating from 1977, we modern Protestants have misunderstood Paul (due to the influence of Luther, who had misunderstood Paul by reading him autobiographically) by first misunderstanding "Second Temple" (really first cen-

20. See David Engelsma, "The Binding of God," *The Trinity Review*, January/February 2002. Oddly, this new view of Calvin is not basically new, but a revival of Perry Miller's fundamental misunderstanding of covenant theology, in which, according to Miller, the doctrine of the covenant was developed in order to warm and soften the cold, hard doctrines of God's eternal predestination and decrees of election and reprobation.

21. See "The Doctrine of Justification in the Theology of Jonathan Edwards," *The Westminster Theological Journal*, Spring 1984, 26-52.

tury A.D.) Judaism as a works-righteousness religion. Once we rid ourselves of that error about Judaism, we can understand justification as Paul and James intended – the key to how Gentiles are now included in the covenant. They enter by faith and baptism, and they maintain their position in the covenant by their faithful obedience. For the past 20 years the pages of *The Westminster Theological Journal* have been peppered with articles by men who espouse some variation of this viewpoint, either in its Shepherd variation or its New Perspective variation: Don Garlington, Joseph Braswell, Richard B. Gaffin, Jr., Peter Leithart, Samuel T. Logan, Jr., John M. Frame, and R. J. Gore, to name several.

Professor Gaffin's appeal to Herman Bavinck is more plausible than the theological revisionism of Calvin that he and Shepherd pioneered in their attempt to find precedent for their views. Appeal to Bavinck is plausible, because Bavinck reveals the profound theological irrationalism that gave rise to Shepherdism in the first place. One should not be surprised if Bavinck's views on justification were confused as well.

His *Doctrine of God* (also translated from the *Gereformeerde Dogmatiek*) begins with a chapter on "God's Incomprehensibility" in which the first paragraph asserts that "the idea that the believer would be able to understand and comprehend intellectually the revealed mysteries is equally unscriptural. On the contrary, the truth which God has revealed concerning himself in nature and in Scripture far surpasses human conception and comprehension. In that sense Dogmatics is concerned with nothing but mystery."[22]

22. Herman Bavinck, *The Doctrine of God*, The Banner of Truth Trust [1918, 1951] 1977, 13. Notice that Bavinck asserts that it is impossible for the "believer" to understand Scripture. His phrase "understand and compre-

Apart from the fact that Bavinck here uses the word "mystery" in a sense not found in Scripture – for in Scripture, mysteries are divine secrets revealed to men for their intellectual understanding and knowledge[23] – Bavinck tells us that we cannot know what we are talking about in theology, for the subject matter of theology "far surpasses human conception."

Bavinck does not shrink from the implications of his theological skepticism, which is a direct attack on divine propositional revelation. He writes for several pages, quoting various medieval theologians with approval:

> Accordingly, adequate knowledge of God does not exist. There is no name that makes known unto us his being. No concept fully embraces him. No description does justice to him. That which is hidden behind the curtain of revelation is entirely unknowable.... Justin Martyr calls God inexpressible, immovable, nameless. The words Father, God, Lord, are not real names "but appellations derived from his good deeds and functions...." "God is known better when not known...."
>
> The fact that God exists is evident, but "what he is in his essence and nature is entirely incomprehensible and unknowable...." When we say that God is unborn, immutable, without beginning, etc., we are only saying what he is *not*. To say what he *is*, is impossible. He is nothing of all that which exists....[24] There is no concept, expression, or word by which God's being can be indicated.

---

hend intellectually" is redundant. By what means, other than the intellect, can we understand and comprehend?

23. See, for example, *Matthew* 13:11, *Mark* 4:11, *Luke* 8:10, *Romans* 11:25, *Romans* 16:25, *1 Corinthians* 2:7ff., *1 Corinthians* 4:1, *1 Corinthians* 13:2, *1 Corinthians* 15:51, *Ephesians* 1:9, and so on.

24. This, of course, is atheism.

Accordingly, when we wish to designate God, we use metaphorical language....[25] We cannot form a conception of that unitary, unknown being, transcendent above all being, above goodness, above every name and word and thought....

Negative theology is better than positive.... Nevertheless, even negative theology fails to give us any knowledge[26] of God's being, for in reality God is exalted above both "negation and affirmation."...[27] "For it is more correct to say that God is not that which is predicated concerning him than to say that he is. He is known better by him who does not know him, whose true ignorance is wisdom...."[28] Indeed, so highly is he exalted above all creatures that the name "nothing" may justly be ascribed to him.... [29]

The statements: "God cannot be defined; he has no name; the finite cannot grasp the infinite," are found in the works of all the theologians. They unanimously affirm that our God is highly exalted above our comprehension, our imagination, and our language.... "Whatever is said concerning God is not God, for God is ineffable...."

There is no knowledge of God as he is in himself.... No name fully expresses his being; no definition describes him. He is exalted infinitely high above our conception, thought, and language.

---

25. This is a denial of literal truth about God.

26. Notice the denial of "any knowledge."

27. If this were so, God and Satan would be indistinguishable.

28. One wonders whether George Orwell had read this statement, since he incorporated it into *1984*. More likely he had read medieval theologians.

29. This is precisely what atheists say of God: God is nothing.

Now, any informed Christian, actually any sane person, reading these pages in *The Doctrine of God*, would stop and lay Bavinck's book aside. The reader has just been told, repeatedly and emphatically, that no thought or language adequately and accurately describes God, that we can have no knowledge of God. If that were so, there would obviously be no point in reading further, unless it is to attain a clinical understanding of how a mind can become so disordered as to write a book on a subject about which he can know and say nothing.

This is the Antichristian irrationalism that passes for Christian theology in both Protestant and Catholic, "conservative" and "liberal" seminaries. It explains the "dialectical," that is, contradictory, pronouncements that issue forth from every modern school of theology. In such a turbid atmosphere, anything goes, including the simultaneous affirmations that justification is by faith alone and also by faith and works. No Christian doctrine, none whatsoever, can be maintained in such a mystical, skeptical, and irrational framework. It is a black hole that swallows and extinguishes all light and all rational thought. It is the medieval mother of all heresies, for the rejection of propositional revelation is the root of all error. Bavinck was a conduit carrying this rubbish into Reformed theology in the twentieth century.

Vantilianism. This writer has some sympathy for those followers of Cornelius Van Til who ignored the warnings about Van Til's philosophy and theology from Gordon Clark and The Trinity Foundation and have now been embarrassed by their mentor's defense of Norman Shepherd, and, in particular, his heretical doctrine of justification. Their embarrassment might have been avoided.

Beginning in the 1940s, Dr. Clark warned the church about the pernicious nature and effect of the dialectical theology and philosophy of Professor Van Til. The Trinity Foundation has published several essays and books on the subject, including *God's Hammer: The Bible and Its Critics; The Clark-Van Til Controversy;* and *Cornelius Van Til: The Man and the Myth.* A few Vantilians listened, but most did not. Now the dialectical Dutch[30] chickens have come home to roost, and their homecoming has become an embarrassment to those Vantilians who unequivocally believe and defend the Gospel of justification by faith alone.

Randy Booth, a Vantilian pastor and author who recently spoke at Shepherdfest 2003, a conference on the covenant sponsored by followers of Vantilian Greg Bahnsen at the Southern California Center for Christian Studies (SCCCS), recently published an essay titled "Caution and Respect in Controversy." In this essay, Booth asserts that "Unsubstantiated charges of heresy have been leveled at both Professor Shepherd and those associated with the AAPC" (3). Now if one reads Palmer Robertson's *Current Justification Controversy*, or recent issues of *The New Southern Presbyterian Review*, or the several essays in *The Trinity Review* on the topic, and more at The Trinity Foundation website, he will find all the substantiation needed to justify the charges against both Shepherd and the Auburn Avenue Presbyterian Church. Booth has apparently failed to do this, and so he asserts, falsely, that these charges are unsubstantiated.

30. Charles Craig, who ran the Presbyterian and Reformed Publishing Company in the 1950s, 1960s, and 1970s, referred to two men he published as "Dutch" and "Double-Dutch": Cornelius Van Til and Herman Dooyeweerd.

What Booth has read is what he presents as "a transcription of a speech by Cornelius Van Til at the Justification Controversy meeting of the Committee of the Whole of the OPC Philadelphia Presbytery" (7). Although he does not date the speech, it was obviously delivered sometime during the Shepherd controversy in the OPC more than 20 years ago. Booth quotes Van Til's speech to support his statements that

> Van Til was, from the beginning and all the way through the Shepherd controversy, an unashamed supporter of Norman Shepherd, as was the majority of the Westminster faculty, including Richard Gaffin and John Frame.... As Van Til vigorously and publicly supported Shepherd, he refuted the errors of those who opposed him, arguing that those opposing Shepherd were attempting to separate faith and works [7].

Booth also quotes John Frame as saying: "Van Til and others, including myself, believed that Shepherd's formulations were orthodox."

Here are Van Til's words, as provided by Booth:

> I think that when we begin with the idea of faith, we have to think first of all that the devils also believe and tremble. Now we have faith by which we need *not* to tremble because Christ on the cross said, "My God, My God, why hast Thou forsaken me?" so that His people might not be forsaken. It is finished! It *was* finished, once for all. Now that is, I think, beautifully expressed in this word of our Lord [discussion of *John* 6:22ff.].
>
> When the multitudes wanted to make Him king because He had given them bread, and they thought it would be easy to have a handout, Jesus said, when they

43

found the other side, "Rabbi, when did you get here?" Jesus said, "Truly I say to you, ye seek me not because ye see signs but because you ate the loaves and were filled." Now then comes the crucial point. "Do not work for food which perishes but for food which endures to eternal life which the Son of Man shall give to you, for of him the Father even God has been sealed." They therefore said, "What shall we do, that we may work the works of God?" Jesus answered and said unto them, "This is the work of God, that ye may believe on Him Whom He hath sent."

Here faith and works are *identical*. Not similar but *identical*. The work *is* faith; faith *is* work. We believe in Jesus Christ and in His salvation, that's why we do not tremble. He *died* for us, in *our* place, and the Scotsmen would say "in our room and stead," for that substitutionary atonement, on the basis of which we are forensically righteous with God and are now righteous in His sight and shall inherit the kingdom of heaven in which *only* the righteous shall dwell. And I'm going to ask John Frame if he will quote the Greek of this particular passage.

[Frame works through it reading both the Greek and English.]

I thank you. Well now, you see faith alone is not alone. Faith *is not* alone. Faith always has an object. The faith, your *act* of believing, is pointed *definitely* to God in Jesus Christ, and by the regeneration of the Holy Spirit, and conversion. It's all one. It's not a "janus-face" [Janus-faced – JR] proposition, but it is not possible to give exhaustive statements in human words, human concepts. And that's why we have to be satisfied merely to do what the Scriptures and confessions of faith say that they [*i.e.*, we] ought to do, and that then we are on the way, and I think that Norman Shepherd is certainly in the line of *direct descent* of [*i.e.*, on the topic of] faith. Thank you. [Emphases noted are Van Til's.]

More important than Van Til's confused, rambling defense of Norman Shepherd is the influence of his thought at Westminster Seminary and in the Orthodox Presbyterian Church from the 1940s to the present. One can see, running through the Shepherd controversy, the influence of Van Til in, for example (1) Shepherd's repeated affirmation of contradictory and conflicting statements, such as that Adam's obedience (had Adam in fact obeyed God's command) would have been meritorious; and Adam's obedience would not have been meritorious;[31] (2) Shepherd's repeated affirmation of the teaching of the Westminster Standards on justification, while at the same time teaching contrary to the Westminster Standards on justification; (3) Shepherd's abuse of the doctrine of the incomprehensibility of God in order to deny to men knowledge revealed in Scripture, in an attempt to justify his contention that "covenantal election" can be lost; (4) Shepherd's assertion of the "free offer of the gospel" – meaning the fictitious doctrine of the sincere desire of God to save all men, elect and reprobate[32] – in order to justify his contention that evangelists should tell every man, "Christ died for you." These are four specific examples; but the influence of the paradoxical, dialectical theology of Van Til pervades Shepherd's thought, as

31. See below, *Reason and Specifications*.

32. This false doctrine was stated and defended by John Murray and Ned Stonehouse in their 1948 essay "The Free Offer of the Gospel." For a refutation, see Garrett Johnson, "The Myth of Common Grace," *The Trinity Review*, March/April 1987. Murray and Stonehouse wrote their essay as part of the Clark-Van Til controversy in the 1940s.

well as the thought of his defenders, who with their "Biblical theology" and "multiperspectivalism,"[33] have turned Reformed theology into a Babel of confusion.

Worse, Van Til's influence is seen not only as the context and form of Shepherd's thought, but also as the context and form of his critics' thought – at least those critics affiliated with Westminster Seminary and the Presbytery of Philadelphia. It is clear from Dr. Robertson's history of the Shepherd controversy[34] that neither the Seminary nor the Presbytery, over a seven-year period, could deal definitively and decisively with the theology of Norman Shepherd. Why not? The Philadelphia Presbytery of the OPC, the Seminary Board, and the Seminary Faculty were paralyzed by the influence of Van Til's dialectical theology, which subverts logical, noncontradictory thought. So when the Executive Committee of the Seminary Board, writing its *Reason and Specifications* explaining why Norman Shepherd was finally dismissed after seven years of discussion, pointed out that "The Faculty report [of February 1977] called attention to the responsibility of teachers to avoid confusing statements," the reminder was not only several decades too late, but contrary to the practice of Westminster's most famous professor, Cornelius Van Til.

For decades, Professor Van Til's stock-in-trade, both in the classroom and in his books, had been confusing statements. Worse, this confusion was not inadvertent; it was deliberate. Van Til had written: "It is precisely because they [the colleagues and followers of Van Til] are concerned to defend the Christian doctrine of revelation as basic to all intelligible human

33. See the works of John Frame and Vern Poythress.

34. See O. Palmer Robertson, *The Current Justification Controversy*. The Trinity Foundation, 2003.

predication that they refuse to make any attempt at 'stating clearly' any Christian doctrine, or the relation of any one Christian doctrine to any other Christian doctrine. They will not attempt to 'solve' the 'paradoxes' involved in the relationship of the self-contained God to his dependent creatures."[35] Notice the four appearances of "any" in that first sentence: They – the Westminster Faculty – refuse to make *any* attempt to state clearly *any* Christian doctrine, or the relation of *any* one Christian doctrine to *any* other Christian doctrine. Furthermore, this is stated as a "refusal": They *refuse* to state clearly any Christian doctrine. It is a deliberate act, not an error of omission or oversight. Furthermore, this refusal is made into a fundamental principle of theology: They refuse to state any doctrine clearly, because such a refusal is fundamental to the whole enterprise of Christian apologetics: "It is precisely because they are concerned to defend the Christian doctrine of revelation." Defending the doctrine of revelation demands that Christian apologists deliberately and principially refuse to state any doctrine clearly, and principially requires them to be confusing.

Professor Van Til practiced what he taught. His unintelligibility was legendary, so much so that it was the object of foolish admiration and jesting. One admiring jest at a Westminster Seminary banquet is recounted by William White, Jr., in his book *Van Til: Defender of the Faith, An Authorized Biography*:

> "There is a controversy today as to who is the greatest intellect of this segment of the twentieth century," the m.c. said. "Probably most thinking people would vote for the learned Dr. Einstein. Not me. I wish to put forth

---

35. Cornelius Van Til, *An Introduction to Systematic Theology*, 172.

as my candidate for the honor, Dr. Cornelius Van Til."
(Loud applause.) "My reason for doing so is this: Only
eleven people in the world understand Albert Einstein....
Nobody – but *nobody* in the world – understands
Cornelius Van Til."[36]

Van Til taught that logical paradox is an ineradicable characteristic of divine revelation, and hence a sign of Christian
spirituality. He wrote, "All teaching of Scripture is apparently
contradictory."[37] That phrase "all teaching" includes, of course,
the doctrine of salvation. So when Norman Shepherd asserts
that faith is the sole instrument of justification, and that works
are also instruments of justification, he is merely following
Van Til's prescription: All teaching of Scripture is apparently
contradictory.

Van Til's writings are peppered with paradoxes, meaningless phrases, undefined terms, and misleading analogies. He
wrote: "Now since God is not fully comprehensible to us we
are bound to come into what seems to be contradiction in all
our knowledge. Our knowledge is analogical and therefore
must be paradoxical."[38] Our knowledge *must* be paradoxical.
It can *never* make sense. So if Professor Shepherd blows hot
and cold, that is a sign of confusion, and therefore of Christian spirituality.

36. William White, Jr., *Van Til: Defender of the Faith*. Thomas Nelson
Publishers, 1979, 181-182.

37. Cornelius Van Til, *Common Grace and Witness Bearing*, 22. At another time, Van Til denied that these paradoxes were merely apparent:
After rejecting Barth's view that contradictions don't matter, he wrote: "Or
shall we with Gordon Clark say that the 'contradiction' that we think we
'see' is no real contradiction at all? We cannot follow any of these ways"
(*Toward a Reformed Apologetics*, 4).

38. Cornelius Van Til, *The Defense of the Faith*, 1967, 44.

As an example of his own contradictory thought, Van Til both affirmed and denied the proofs for the existence of God. He wrote: "I do not reject the 'theistic proofs' but merely insist on formulating them in such a way as not to compromise the doctrines of Scripture. 'That is to say, if the theistic proof is constructed as it ought to be constructed, it is objectively valid....' "[39] On the other hand, he also wrote, "Of course Reformed believers do not seek to prove the existence of their God. To seek to prove or to disprove the existence of this God would be to deny him.... A God whose existence is 'proved' is not the God of Scripture."[40]

Van Til's disdain for "mere human logic" was well-known. He warned about squeezing the events of history into the forms of logic: "We fall into logicism. We reduce the significance of the stream of history to the static categories of logic."[41] We hear the echoes of this phrase ("the static categories of logic") in the Neolegalists: Norman Shepherd and his disciples, Douglas Wilson, Steven Schlissel, Steven Wilkins, Andrew Sandlin, John Barach, and so on. They contrast the "static categories of God's decrees" with the "covenant dynamic." They decry "rationalism," "logicism," and "gnosticism." They assert the inadequacy of human language to express divine truth, and the futility of using human logic to understand it. But the Second Person of the Trinity, the *Logos*, had no difficulty expressing divine truth in the human languages of Aramaic, Greek, and Hebrew while he walked on Earth; and the Third Person, the Holy Spirit, wrote the perfect, completely accurate, fully adequate, and inerrant Scriptures in human language.

39. Cornelius Van Til, *The Defense of the Faith*, 1967, 197.
40. Cornelius Van Til, *The Protestant Doctrine of Scripture*, 1967, 137.
41. Cornelius Van Til, *An Introduction to Systematic Theology*, 256.

The Vantilians' disdain for systematic thought, their preference for "Biblical theology" (which is not Biblical at all), which frees its practitioners from the constraints of logic and allows them to interpret Scripture willy-nilly, without regard to context[42] or other passages of Scripture, is a result of their disdain for "mere human logic." Writing of the statement in chapter 1, paragraph 6, of the *Westminster Confession* that "The whole counsel of God, concerning all things necessary for his own glory, man's salvation, faith, and life, is either expressly set down in Scripture, or by good and necessary consequence may be deduced from Scripture," Van Til said: *"This statement should not be used as a justification for deductive exegesis."*[43] But deductive exegesis is precisely what this Confessional statement endorses. In fact, correct exegesis is impossible without using logical deduction.

Norman Shepherd's subversion of chapter 11 of the *Westminster Confession* on Justification both depends upon and is required by Cornelius Van Til's subversion of chapter 1 of the *Westminster Confession*, on Scripture. In many ways, perhaps not in all, Norman Shepherd is the theological child of Van Til, working out in the field of soteriology Van Til's philosophical rejection of rational, systematic, noncontradictory revelation. It is not unexpected that those who begin with a medieval denial of divine propositional revelation – such as one finds in Bavinck's *Doctrine of God* – end with a medieval doctrine of salvation.

42. See, for example, Richard Gaffin's and Norman Shepherd's misinterpretation of *Romans* 2:13, without regard to its context or Paul's argument in *Romans* 1-3.

43. Cornelius Van Til, *A Christian Theory of Knowledge*, 1969, 38. Emphasis is Van Til's.

The fundamental problem with the theories of Bavinck, Van Til, and Shepherd is that divine revelation is given in human words, so human words and concepts are *ipso facto* adequate to express, discuss, and ponder all the divine truth that God has given to us. To deny that is to deny divine revelation *in toto*.

The Dark Age views of Bavinck and Van Til on language, logic, and the knowledge of God are so radically Antichristian that they subvert all Christian doctrine. The doctrine of salvation was not the first doctrine to be corrupted by this irrationalism, which is a revival of the mysticism of the Dark Ages, nor will it be the last. The rejection of literal, propositional truth about God, the assertion that human language cannot express divine truth adequately or accurately, the rejection of "mere human logic," the assertion that God is beyond "affirmation and negation," are denials of the first principle of Christianity, which is literal, propositional revelation from God, given in human language and propositions, using human logic.

The *Westminster Confession of Faith* recognizes Scripture as the first principle of Christianity by placing the doctrine of Scripture in its first and longest chapter. All the rest of Christianity – all 32 subsequent chapters of the *Confession* – rest on the foundation of Scripture alone. Nothing is to be added to or removed from Scripture.

In its first chapter, the *Confession*, quoting Scripture itself, asserts the infallibility and sufficiency – not the inadequacy and inaccuracy – of the human words God himself spoke in Scripture. The *Confession*, echoing Scripture itself, asserts that Scripture is to be studied and understood, not blindly accepted. The *Confession*, echoing Scripture itself, asserts that logical deduction – "good and necessary consequence" – is the principal tool of understanding Scripture. Logical deduction must be used to compare Scripture with Scripture, for Scripture is its own infallible interpreter – it does not need pope, priest, seminary professor, or psychologist in order to be understood.

Bavinck's and Van Til's view of language and logic is a rejection of the doctrine of Scripture. Rather than the inerrancy, infallibility, sufficiency, clarity, and authority of Scripture, their view asserts the inadequacy, inaccuracy, insufficiency, and murkiness of Scripture, to the point that, to quote Bavinck,

> adequate knowledge of God does not exist. There is no name that makes known unto us his being.... The words Father, God, Lord are not real names.... what he is in his essence and nature is entirely incomprehensible and unknowable.... To say what he is, is impossible.... There is no concept, expression, or word by which God's being can be indicated.... We cannot form a conception of that unitary, unknown being....even negative theology fails to give us any knowledge of God's being....Whatever is said concerning God is not God.... There is no knowledge of God as he is in himself....

Bavinck's and Van Til's view of language and logic is a rejection of the Christian doctrine of God, for God is omnipotent, and he is able to speak – and he has spoken in Scripture, in human words – exactly what he intends to say. Far from being hampered by human logic and language, God reveals himself as he is by human logic and language.

Bavinck's and Van Til's view of language and logic is a rejection of the doctrine of the Incarnation, for the Second Person of the Trinity, the *Logos*, became man, and expressed his divine thoughts in human words, using human logic and categories. Jesus Christ spoke and wrote Aramaic, Hebrew, and Greek, and the human words he spoke and wrote expressed his meaning perfectly.

Bavinck's and Van Til's view of language and logic is a rejection of the doctrine of man's creation in God's image, for God created Adam and gave Adam the gifts of language and logic so that he might talk to God, and God might talk to him. Communion with God was then and is still intellectual communion. That is why the Apostle Paul says of believers: "We have the mind of Christ."

Bavinck approvingly quoted medieval theologians attacking the Christian doctrine of revelation. The anti-theology he and they espouse led, and will always lead, to a Dark Age, when the light of God's Word and Gospel are virtually lost. The current and growing rejection of the Gospel of justification by faith alone is one result of that rejection of divine, literal, propositional revelation. That rejection is the heresy matrix, the source of all error and heresies.

Now that we have looked at some of the roots of Neolegalism in Reformed churches, it is time to look, briefly, at some of the fruits of this movement. Let's begin with the recent case of John O. Kinnaird.

The Kinnaird Case. John Kinnaird is a Ruling Elder in the Orthodox Presbyterian Church. He was an avid defender of Norman Shepherd during the Shepherd controversy. In 2002 and 2003, Kinnaird was tried for and convicted of teaching a doctrine of justification by faith and works, contrary to the Scriptures and the *Westminster Confession.* That conviction by the Session of Bethany Presbyterian Church (OPC), was upheld by the Presbytery of Philadelphia in the OPC, and then struck down by the General Assembly of the OPC in June 2003.

Here are excerpts from the teaching of Elder Kinnaird that the General Assembly of the OPC has declared to be acceptable and Biblical:

> Why do people need to be sanctified and glorified? The answer is that when Adam sinned, he and all descending from him (WCF VI.3) lost the righteousness wherein mankind was created and, thereby, mankind also lost communion with God. If communion with God is to be restored, righteousness of a real and personal nature must be restored.

According to Kinnaird, it is our "real and personal righteousness" that "restores communion with God," not the perfect imputed righteousness of Christ.

He continues:

> God has appointed a day when he will judge the world in righteousness. All persons who have lived upon the earth shall appear before the tribunal of Christ to give account of their thoughts, words, and deeds; and to receive according to what they have done in the body, whether good or bad. On That Great Day of Judgement [sic], God's righteous judgement will be revealed. God will then give to each person according to what he has done. To those who by persistence in doing good (we Presbyterians call this perseverance) seek glory, honor, and immortality, he will give eternal life. For those who are self-seeking and who reject the truth and follow evil, there will be eternal wrath and anger (Romans 2:6-8) and destruction from before the face of the Lord. It is

those who obey the law who will be declared righteous on that Day of Judgment.

Note that Kinnaird says the judgment according to works will decide whether one receives eternal life or death. Those who will be "declared righteous," that is justified, and given eternal life will be "those who obey the law." He is not discussing degrees of reward, but salvation and damnation. In fact, he explicitly denies he is discussing degrees of reward:

> Those who teach that the purpose of the Day of Judgement [sic] is not to reveal God's righteousness in his judgements (judgements that will be unto eternal life or death in accord with what men have done on this earth), but rather only to determine types and degrees of rewards to be given to Christians, are in error.

Kinnaird continues, echoing Shepherd:

> These good works are a required condition if we would stand in the Day of Judgment and they are supplied by God to all His people. Every description of the Judgment events speaks of these good works. Without them, no one will see God.... Who are these people who thus benefit – who stand on the Day of Judgment? They are those who obey the law who will be declared righteous.

Good works are a "required condition" of salvation. The imputed righteousness of Christ is insufficient. Those who will be "declared righteous," that is, justified, will be "those who obey the law."

Again Kinnaird:

> It is not possible that any could be a brother to Jesus Christ and enjoy with Christ in the Kingdom of Heaven,

the presence of God the Father except that one be fully conformed to the image of Christ in true and personal righteousness and holiness. Neither the imputation of the righteousness of Christ, which all Christians receive at justification, nor the infusion of the righteousness of Christ (a false and non-existent concept taught by the Roman Catholic Church) can suffice for that purpose. Christ does not have an imputed righteousness. His righteousness is real and personal. If we are to be conformed to his image, we too must have a real and personal righteousness.

Kinnaird asserts that the imputed righteousness of Christ cannot suffice for making us brothers of Christ or allowing us to stand in the presence of God. Kinnaird makes our "real and personal righteousness" sufficient for both those things – adoption and communion with God. Among other things, his language suggests that Christ's imputed righteousness is not "real."

> On the Day of Judgement [sic] I will hear God declare me to be righteous. As to the reason for that, it is not because of the works, even though it will be in accord with the works. The reason will be: first, because it [God's declaration that John Kinnaird is righteous] will be true because God will have changed me so that I am really and personally righteous. After all, we will be crowned with righteousness. This is the result of the work of the Holy Spirit in my sanctification in this life.

According to Kinnaird, God's declaration of righteousness is not made because of the imputed righteousness of Christ, but because "God will have changed me so that I am really and personally righteous." Had God not changed Kinnaird, such a declaration of righteousness presumably would not have been true. Kinnaird will be declared righteous because of his sanctification and the work of the Holy Spirit, not because of the imputed, alien righteousness of Christ. The imputed righteousness of Christ is depreciated in Kinnaird's soteriology, for he apparently thinks imputed righteousness is unreal and impersonal: He always contrasts it unfavorably with a righteousness that is "real" and "personal."

After the OPC General Assembly had overturned Kinnaird's conviction and found his teachings acceptable, ten Commissioners to the General Assembly signed a Protest against the decision. Among other things, the Protest declares:

> The decision of the Assembly to sustain the appeal opens the gate, in the judgment of the undersigned, to the use throughout the Orthodox Presbyterian Church of a hermeneutic that allows interpretations of Scripture that are out of accord with the whole body of the Word.

This writer applauds the Protest, and prays that there will be an overwhelming reaction in the OPC against this decision, and a return to the Gospel of Jesus Christ. But the hermeneutical gate to Antichristian interpretations of Scripture was opened long ago in the OPC. Indeed, it is the prevalence of this irrational, dialectical hermeneutic that permitted this decision to be made. To change the metaphor, the cancer that has long been present in the OPC and at Westminster Seminary has metastasized.

To pretend that the Kinnaird case has no connection to the Shepherd case, as some have alleged, is to deceive only oneself. John O. Kinnaird has long been associated with Norman

Shepherd and has defended him publicly. The OPC failed to deal with Shepherd's views properly 25 years ago, and now his proteges and sympathizers apparently control that denomination and Westminster Seminary. Richard B. Gaffin, Jr., is a stalwart defender of both Norman Shepherd and John Kinnaird. Gaffin filed a Complaint against the action of the Presbytery of Philadelphia in upholding Bethany OPC Session's conviction of Kinnaird for teaching justification by faith and works. Gaffin also spoke in Shepherd's behalf at the OPC General Assembly.

Still another name that reappeared in the Kinnaird case is G. I. Williamson, who wrote a letter praising Norman Shepherd (Dr. Robertson quotes it in *The Current Justification Controversy*) during the Shepherd controversy, and who favored John Kinnaird during his appeal at the OPC General Assembly in June 2003.[44]

The Auburn Avenue Presbyterian Church. The Session of the Auburn Avenue Presbyterian Church (PCA) in Monroe, Louisiana, has been a proponent of Neolegalism for years. Its policy of aggressively promoting false doctrine finds expression not only through its worship, which includes the use of kneelers, and distinctive clothing for its leaders; but also through Pastors Conferences; a nationally distributed church newsletter, *The Auburn Analecta*; its "Dabney Institute;" and the widespread distribution of tapes. Led by J. Steven Wilkins, the AAPC Session invited Norman Shepherd to speak at its 2002 Pastors Conference, but due to the death of his wife, Shepherd's understudy John Barach substituted for him.

44. To read the documents in the Kinnaird case, go to www.trinityfoundation.org, and click on "Kinnaird."

Shepherd is scheduled to lecture on justification at the AAPC in October 2003, apparently in dishonor of Luther and the Reformation.[45] Now the AAPC is soliciting $200,000 to set up a publishing company to promote its false theology by publishing books.

The April 28, 2003 issue of *Christian Renewal*, a Canadian newspaper, carried an interview with Steven Wilkins, Douglas Wilson, John Barach, and Steven Schlissel. These four men have been in the vanguard of Neolegalism within the PCA and other "Reformed" denominations. Douglas Wilson, for example, is pastor of Christ Church and head of New St. Andrews College, both in Moscow, Idaho, where Peter Leithart and Douglas Jones teach. Of course, these are not the only spokesmen for Neolegalism. One might also visit the website of PCA minister Mark Horne, an avid promoter of the views of Norman Shepherd and N. T. Wright, or the website of John Knox Presbyterian Church (PCA) in Ruston, Louisiana (www.johnknoxpca.org). There are many more sympathizers with these men who are not spokesmen for Neolegalism, but who defend these men against criticism. They provide the sea in which the sharks swim.

The *Christian Renewal* interview with Wilkins, Schlissel, Wilson, and Barach[46] reeks of hostility toward systematic thought, asserts sacramentarianism, and further corroborates what their critics have said: These men do not teach – in fact

---

45. Next March, the misnamed Reformation and Revival Ministries (headed by John Armstrong) and the Center for Cultural Leadership (headed by Andrew Sandlin), have scheduled an ecumenical Conference on Law and Gospel at which Shepherd, Steve Schlissel, Don Garlington, and a Roman and an Orthodox priest, among others, are scheduled to speak.

46. *Christian Renewal*, April 28, 2003, 11-14.

they reject, as clearly as their deliberately unsystematic thinking will allow – the Gospel of Jesus Christ.

Steven Schlissel, pastor of Messiah's Congregation in
Brooklyn, New York, and editor of a new book praising Greg
Bahnsen, denies the difference between Law and Gospel, call-
ing it imaginary:

> Have Reformed folks gotten it wrong? Yes, to the ex-
> tent that they've followed Luther in an imaginary Law/
> Gospel antithesis.... The law as God gave it is the gos-
> pel.... And the gospel as announced by Paul is the
> law....The gospel brings demands.... The gospel has ob-
> ligations. Always has.... the gospel is permeated with
> God's good law.

Schlissel asserts that sinners can keep the law of God, and
by keeping it, they will be saved:

> Rather it was Christ's teaching [in *Luke* 10:25-28] that
> obedience to the law was something very do-able and
> that such obedience, which includes repentance and
> faith, does save.... In *Luke* 18 we have no hint of a faith
> vs. works dichotomy, or law vs. grace. Rather we have
> Jesus pressing the law as containing that which leads to
> eternal life.

Schlissel denies that justification is by faith apart from works:
"...we insist that saving faith is an obedient faith." Some reader
may ask, What is wrong with that? Isn't saving faith obedient?
The Biblical response is that faith saves "apart from works."
We are not justified by faith-together-with-works, but by faith-
apart-from-works, as Paul says repeatedly. Mere faith, mere
belief, is what saves, and works flow from that belief. Works
are the result of salvation already possessed, not a condition

of salvation yet to be received. Obedience does not make faith saving. Faith alone is saving.

Schlissel endorses Norman Shepherd: "...at the same time a truly Reformed Westminster [Confession] subscriber such as Norman Shepherd can't even be mentioned there [Westminster Seminary]. But the Baptists are accepted."

Douglas Wilson also denies justification by faith alone:

> What drives apostasy is unbelief, and the engine that drives salvation is faith and only faith.
> [Interviewer: But not faith only?]
> Not bare bones faith. Not assent. Devils have that. True faith is more than assent.... we say faith cannot be separated from trust and obedience, and...we say saving faith cannot be separated from a life of obedience and trust.

Of course, this is a denial of Paul's explicit statement that it is belief, "apart from works," any and all works, that justifies. Paul does exactly what Wilson says cannot be done: He separates faith from works. Any message that does not do this is not the Gospel.

Steven Wilkins asserts that everyone who is baptized is raised to newness of life, but the baptized person can lose that new life if his response to God is not good enough:

> *Romans* 6 says that we've been baptized into Christ and his death, burial and resurrection and raised to newness of life. That's objectively true of everyone who receives baptism. That doesn't mean that they are saved no matter how they live or respond to the grace of God. Indeed, Paul warns them about the possibility of being cut off because of arrogance and unbelief in *Romans* 11.
> [Interviewer: Can we be in the church but not united to Christ?]

That's a distinction the Bible doesn't make...the distinction is not biblical. The visible, historic church is the body of Christ, and thus to be joined to it by baptism is to be united to Christ. By baptism God offers and gives Christ to us....

John Barach echoes this thought in one of his lectures:

Every baptized person is in covenant with God and is in union with Christ and with the triune God. The Bible doesn't know about a distinction between being internally in the covenant – really in the covenant – and being only externally in the covenant, just being in the sphere of the covenant. The Bible speaks about the reality, efficacy, of baptism. Every baptized person is in Christ and therefore shares in His new life.... We need to say Jesus died for you personally and we mean it, to them, head for head, every one of them.[47]

The Summary Statement adopted by the Session of the Auburn Avenue Presbyterian Church develops this idea further:

By baptism one is joined to Christ's body, united to him covenantally, and *given all the blessings and benefits of his work*.... This does not, however, grant to the baptized final salvation;[48] rather it obligates him to fulfill the terms of the covenant....[49] In some sense, they [bap-

---

47. John Barach, "Covenant and History," Tape 3.

48. This means, of course, that "final salvation" is not one of the "benefits and blessings" of Christ's work, for every baptized person receives "all the benefits and blessings of Christ's work," but not every baptized person is finally saved. Thus the Auburn theology is a direct attack on Christ and the sufficiency of his perfect work – a direct denial of the Gospel.

49. This means that "final salvation" is received only after one has satisfactorily performed all the obligations of the covenant. Final salvation is

tized persons] were *really joined* to the elect people, *really sanctified* by Christ's blood, *really recipients* of new life given by the Holy Spirit....[50] Some persons, not destined for final salvation, will be drawn to Christ and His people only for a time. *These, for a season, enjoy real blessings, purchased for them by Christ's cross and applied to them by the Holy Spirit through Word and Sacrament....* Saul received the *same initial covenantal grace* that David, Gideon, and other men who persevered in faith received, but he did not receive the gift of perseverance....[51]

Wilkins misunderstands *Titus* 3:5 and teaches baptismal regeneration:

If we mean by regeneration a gift of new life that will never die out but produces persevering faith, then no, I don't believe that is necessarily given at baptism. But I don't believe that is how the Bible uses the term *regeneration*. Take *Titus* 3:5. It says God saves us according to his mercy by means of the washing of regeneration and the renewal of the Holy Ghost. The word washing plainly refers to baptism. Paul says that this washing is some-

---

not received because of Christ's perfect obedience and death. The Auburn theology changes the covenant of grace into a covenant of works, in which the sinner must perform good works in order to be finally saved.

50. Thus all baptized persons are "really joined," "really sanctified," and "really recipients of new life" in Christ. But they will not all be finally saved. Some will be cut off, will become reprobate, and will lose the new life given them by the Holy Spirit, because their works are lacking.

51. This means, of course, that perseverance is not one of the blessings and benefits of Christ's work, for all baptized persons receive all those blessings and benefits. (Emphasis added.) *Summary Statement of the Auburn Avenue Presbyterian Church's Position on the Covenant, Baptism, and Salvation.*

thing that results in regeneration and renewal by the Holy Spirit. It seems plain to me that Paul was not operating with our definition of regeneration. It seems to me that our theological definition is too narrow at this point....

Wilkins simply does not know what Paul says in *Titus* 3:5. I shall let Gordon Clark explain:

Our present text [*Titus* 3:5] now says that God saved us by the washing of regeneration (*palingenesis*). This phrase too excludes past and future works, for clearly it is God who washes, and we are passively washed.

What is this washing?.... No doubt the word *washing* suggests baptism. (It does not suggest immersion.) Nevertheless one can hardly explain the whole passage in terms of baptism. This should be all the more avoided in order to show that the passage does not teach baptismal regeneration.

[At this point Clark quotes two liberal commentators who interpret this passage to teach baptismal regeneration. Then he resumes.]

In reply to this sacramentarianism several points are pertinent. First, let us ask whether the language is figurative or literal. This is a difficult question and incapable of solution if we attend only to the wording of a single sentence. Presumably everyone would acknowledge that "I am the door" is a figure of speech. But "this is my body" has generated endless controversy.... Calvinists, of course, consider *body* to be a metaphorical expression. And why not? When Paul says that the church is the *body* of Christ, can anyone take it literally? Some conservative exegetes take "I am the truth" to be figurative. The present writer to their dismay regards it as philosophically and theologically literal. We must therefore go beyond such phrases in isolation and fit them into the Scriptural system as a whole. Scripture must be interpreted by Scripture.

A second consideration, confined to the verse itself, is that if baptism caused, or was, regeneration, the phrase should have been "the regeneration of washing." The actual phrase "the washing of regeneration" indicates that regeneration washes, not that washing regenerates.

A third point... is that if baptism regenerates, and baptism alone, then Paul was regenerated, not when he saw Christ on the Damascus road, but after Ananias had come to visit him. Perhaps this could be stubbornly maintained, but only by denying that regeneration is a subjective change. Surely Paul "changed his mind," that is, repented, and became a "new man" before he reached the city. Similarly the thief on the cross was regenerated, but never baptized. But if baptism is regeneration, the thief could not have been in Paradise with Christ that evening.

Some defenders of sacramentarianism, if not stubbornly, at least confusedly, deny that regeneration is a subjective change of mind.... [But] the washing effected by regeneration is the renewal, that is, the renewing the Spirit does to us....[52]

In keeping with his sacramentarianism, Wilkins asserts the inseparability of water baptism and Spirit baptism:

Interviewer: Can you be baptized by water and not baptized by the Spirit?

52. Gordon H. Clark, *The Pastoral Epistles.* The Trinity Foundation [1984] 1999, 166-168.

> I would say no. We may distinguish the work of the
> Spirit from baptism, but we should never separate the
> two.... Every time we referred to baptism in the [Pas-
> tors] conference, we would deny that baptism brings
> automatic or infallible salvation. Faith is required of all
> who are joined to Christ in covenant. But we must not
> separate the work of the Spirit from the visible elements
> of the sacrament...though we may distinguish between
> the work of the Spirit and the application of water in
> baptism, we must not separate the two. When we do so,
> we become baptistic.

Now this argument implies that water baptism grants the gift of faith – indeed, as we have seen, the Summary State-ment adopted by the Auburn Avenue Presbyterian Church Session says that all the baptized receive all the benefits and blessings of Christ's work, and those benefits and blessings surely include faith. So what Wilkins seems to be saying here is that while water baptism itself does not save, water bap-tism grants the gift of faith, which does save, but does not "finally save."

Wilkins also misunderstands what makes a marriage – the intelligent, rational consent of the parties, not a ritual – and applies his misunderstanding of marriage to baptism, garbling the doctrine of baptism twice as badly:

> It's [baptism] like a wedding. There is a transforma-
> tion that takes place because of the ritual. A single man
> becomes a married man. He is transformed into a new
> man, with new blessings and privileges and responsi-
> bilities he didn't have before. A similar thing happens at
> baptism. The one who is baptized is transferred from
> the kingdom of darkness into the kingdom of light, from

Adam into Christ, and given new privileges, blessings, and responsibilities he didn't have before.

Wilkins denies that election is a basis of assurance of salvation, and asserts that baptism, which, in contrast to election, is "objective and certain," is the basis of assurance of salvation:

> The decree of election is no ground [of assurance] since no one can know if they [*sic*] have been chosen for salvation. Men must have something objective and certain. But if you refuse to look to your baptism then all you are left with is [subjective] experience....

The doctrine of election, Wilkins says, is "no ground" of assurance. He says that there are only two such possible grounds of assurance, baptism and "subjective experience," and Wilkins dismisses subjective experience as useless. In contrast to Wilkins' view, here is what the *Westminster Confession of Faith* says about the grounds of assurance:

> This certainty [of assurance] is not a bare conjectural and probable persuasion, grounded upon a fallible hope, but an infallible assurance of faith, founded upon the divine truth of the promises of salvation, the inward evidence of those graces unto which these promises are made, the testimony of the Spirit of adoption witnessing with our spirits that we are the children of God; which Spirit is the earnest of our inheritance, whereby we are sealed to the day of redemption.[53]

There is nothing in the *Confession* about being assured of one's salvation by one's baptism. Instead, the *Confession* points

---

53. Chapter 18, section 2.

to the divine truth of the promises of Scripture, and our own belief of the Gospel as grounds of assurance. Furthermore, it is a bizarre mystery why Wilkins thinks baptism would reassure anyone, since he has already admitted that not all those baptized will finally be saved. "Final salvation" depends not on one's baptism, but on one's performance after baptism. If one does not perform satisfactorily, then one will lose one's election, justification, and salvation. In Wilkins' theology, baptism cannot be the ground of assurance of "final salvation" at all.

Wilkins asserts that baptism, not repentance or belief, is what unites us to Christ:

> Paul said you [that is, all the baptized] are all baptized into Christ and members of Christ's body, each of you – no qualifications. He doesn't say, if you sincerely repent of your sins and sincerely believe in Christ, then you're a member of the body.

Not only does Wilkins deny *sola fide*; here he asserts the dispensability of faith altogether, so long as one is baptized. Water baptism unites us to Christ.

Wilkins asserts that we ought to tell each man: "Christ died for you":

> We don't have to know the decrees [of God] to state these covenantal, objective realities very plainly and without qualification. Our [Reformed] theology, focusing as it does upon the decrees of God, has made us fearful of saying something that might eventually be contradicted by God's decrees. Thus, we don't want to say, "Christ died for you," in case God actually didn't ordain the death of Christ to apply to that particular individual. Paul wasn't hampered in this way.

Well, if Paul wasn't hampered in this way, there must be at least one example, and one would think many examples, of Paul's telling unsaved individuals, "Christ died for you." Wilkins fails to cite any.

Nearly 60 years ago, in the 1940s, Herman Hoeksema, writing about the Clark-Van Til controversy in the Orthodox Presbyterian Church, pointed out the latent Arminianism of the Westminster Faculty in their doctrine of the "free offer of the Gospel." Near the end of his commentary, after reviewing the many errors of Van Til and his colleagues, Hoeksema quotes them saying, "The supreme importance for evangelism of maintaining the Reformed doctrine of the Gospel as a universal and sincere offer of salvation is self-evident." Then he asks:

> Do they, in this statement, not reveal their real intention? They first claimed that the Reformed doctrine of the Gospel honors the paradox, the contradiction: God wills to save all men; he wills to save only the elect. Must they, then, not preach that paradox, if they would proclaim the full Gospel, according to their own contention? Must they not do justice to that Gospel, and hide nothing of it, whether in "evangelistic" work or in the ministry of the Word in the Church?
>
> But no; here they tacitly admit that, for evangelistic purposes, their paradoxical gospel is not suitable. And so they propose to forget the one side of their paradox, and to present the Gospel only as a "universal and sincere offer of salvation." And that means that they intend to limit themselves to the proclamation that God sincerely seeks the salvation of all men.

In practice, they intend to preach an Arminian gospel.[54]

In the *Christian Renewal* interview John Barach asserts that we can tell every baptized person that sin has no dominion over him and that God has chosen him for salvation:

> That's [Wilkins' statement about baptism being like a wedding ritual] why we can say to each person, "Sin has no domination over you anymore (*Romans* 6:14). You are now under Christ's Lordship. You've been brought into a new relationship."
>
> The point is that Paul isn't merely speaking about the elect [in 2 *Thessalonians* 2]; he's speaking to the congregation. And we should follow his example. We should say to the church, "Brothers, God chose you for salvation."

Barach also asserts (thus tying the attack on justification to an attack on Scripture) that the Bible is not primarily a sourcebook of theology, but a liturgical book: "But the Bible is not primarily a sourcebook for theology. It's a covenantal book, a liturgical book, a book to be addressed to the church."

In these quotes, we can see a logically incoherent theology – incoherent because it rejects systematic thought – that denies the Gospel. If its proponents become more consistent in their thinking, they will realize – as some of their more intelligent followers have already realized – that they are not the courageous theological pioneers offering the church a "new paradigm" that they think they are. As they round that last curve on their spiritual journey they will see Mother Kirk

---

54. Herman Hoeksema, *The Clark Van Til Controversy*. The Trinity Foundation, 1995, 66-67.

standing there in all her gaudy splendor, her purple and red robes cascading to the ground, her arms outstretched and ready to receive them at last, her lost and wandering children coming home to Rome.

The AAPC Session has published essays written by Roman Catholics and Anglicans in its church newsletter. Among those essays are excerpts from a lecture by N. T. Wright, Bishop of Durham (England) in the apostate Anglican Church, titled "Paul's Gospel and Caesar's Empire." (At the time of his lecture, Bishop Wright was a "Dean" in the Anglican Church; earlier this year he was named Bishop by the Queen, who is the head of the Church of England.) Wright, who is a leading figure in both the "New Perspective on Paul" and the "Quest for the Historical Jesus" movements, is becoming more popular in the PCA and the OPC. Some churches are showing his videotapes; others are promoting his views in print.

The Auburn Avenue Presbyterian Church Session thought so highly of Wright's statements on the Gospel that they excerpted them from a longer lecture and republished them in their church newsletter – statements such as this: "when [the Apostle Paul] referred to 'the gospel,' he was not talking about a scheme of soteriology."

Now soteriology, of course, is that branch of theology that concerns the doctrine of salvation. According to Bishop Wright and *The Auburn Analecta*, when the Apostle Paul speaks in Scripture of "the gospel," he is not referring to a plan of salvation, as Christians have always understood Paul to mean. Rather than salvation from sin and Hell, Paul had something else in mind, Bishop Wright says. (This explains why Bishop Wright titled one of his books *What Saint Paul Really Said.*)

Furthermore, according to Bishop Wright, as published in *The Auburn Analecta*, the phrase "the gospel" never denotes justification by faith: "despite the way Protestantism has used the phrase ["the gospel"] (making it denote, as it never does in Paul, the doctrine of justification by faith...."

Now, if Protestantism is in error, and the Gospel is not about a plan of salvation and justification by faith, what do Bishop Wright and his publishers, the AAPC Session, think the Gospel is about? Bishop Wright answered that question in *The Auburn Analecta*, October 1, 2002: "Paul's proclamation clearly carried a political message at its heart, not merely as one 'implication' among many." Paul's Gospel, according to Bishop Wright writing in *The Auburn Analecta*, is not about a plan of salvation, never means justification by faith, and is, in fact, a political message.

Contrary to what Bishop Wright says in *The Auburn Analecta*, Paul quite clearly did use the phrase "the Gospel" to refer to soteriology and justification by faith: "For I am not ashamed of the Gospel of Christ, for it is the power of God to salvation for everyone who believes, for the Jew first and also for the Greek. For in it [the Gospel] the righteousness of God is revealed from faith to faith: As it is written, 'The just shall live by faith'" (*Romans* 1:16-17). Paul clearly says the Gospel of Jesus Christ is about soteriology, salvation, and justification by faith. The Gospel is not a "political message at its heart." Protestantism is not in error on this point.

By denying what the Apostle Paul clearly says about the Gospel, and by substituting for the Gospel of Christ a political message, both Bishop Wright and his publishers, the AAPC Session, are preaching a false gospel.

Dr. Sidney Dyer, a Professor on the faculty of Greenville

(South Carolina) Presbyterian Theological Seminary, published a review in Greenville Seminary's theological journal of *What Saint Paul Really Said*, one of Bishop Wright's many books. Dr. Dyer had this to say about Bishop Wright's theology:

> The most disturbing material in Wright's book is that which sets forth his view of justification. His effort to take the doctrine out of the realm of soteriology and to put it in the realm of ecclesiology is undoubtedly motivated by his desire to tear down what divides Evangelicals and Roman Catholics.
>
> His view of justification is an attack on the very heart of the Gospel. Paul warned of the danger of preaching another gospel in *Galatians* 1:8, "But if we, or an angel from Heaven, preach any other gospel to you than what we have preached, let him be accursed." Paul, by using the words "*any* other gospel" (emphasis added), shows that he is attacking all other forms of the Gospel....
>
> Wright's view of justification is an attempt to reverse the Reformation. We must resist such attempts. The issue is one of life and death – eternal life and eternal death. When theological professors and pastors abandon the Biblical and Confessional doctrine of justification, they sacrifice the Gospel and the souls of men.[55]

There is one result of this justification controversy that I have not mentioned yet. By God's grace, it is causing many to study the doctrine of salvation all over again, and starting to call forth new statements and defenses of the doctrine of justification by faith alone.

55. Sidney D. Dyer, "N. T. Wright's View of Justification: An Ecumenical Interpretation of Paul," *Katekomen*, Summer 2002, 17ff.

Essential to this work are two books by Gordon H. Clark: *The Johannine Logos* and *Faith and Saving Faith,* in which Clark, rather than repeating the traditional psychological analysis of faith (which is dependent on an un-Scriptural faculty psychology), demonstrates what Scripture means by *faith,* thus closing the back door through which much of this Neolegalism has entered the churches: the notions that saving faith is different from belief, and more than belief, and that it is "commitment" as well. That notion of "commitment" was used by those who confusedly or deliberately set forth a view of justification that denied *sola fide.*

I cannot urge the reader too strongly to study Dr. Clark's two books, for there you will find exegesis that simply cannot be found elsewhere. Theologians have sometimes assumed that "everybody knows" what faith is, so they do not study how Scripture uses the words *believe* and *belief.* The current crisis in the churches is one indication that "everybody" does not know what faith is, and that it is time to learn.

All these streams of thought – Biblical theology, Reconstructionism, the New Perspective on Paul, Shepherdism, Roman Catholicism, Gaffin and Bavinck, Vantilianism and Neoorthodoxy – have contributed to the flood of Neolegalism in the churches. It would be incorrect to single out Norman Shepherd as the cause of our present calamity. But this much we can say: When they had the opportunity and the duty to do so, both Westminster Seminary and the Orthodox Presbyterian Church failed to preserve, protect, and defend the Gospel of Jesus Christ against its enemies. Now a new generation is called to be faithful to their Lord and his truth. In order to be faithful, it must repudiate not only Neolegalism, but the matrix of irrationalism – exemplified in the books of Herman Bavinck and Cornelius Van Til – that gave it birth.

Heresies must come, say the Holy Spirit and the Apostle Paul, but woe to them by whom they come. While heresies always have a deleterious effect on some, God uses them to clarify doctrine, to separate his people from clever counterfeits, to show who has his Gospel and his approval, and to purify his churches. Those advancing new paradigms of salvation are revealed for what they are – errorists in doctrine, who have departed from the faith once delivered to the saints.

The Sanders/Dunn "Fork in the Road" in the Current Controversy over the Pauline Doctrine of Justification by Faith

Robert L. Reymond

The Sanders/Dunn "Fork in the Road" in the Current Controversy over the Pauline Doctrine of Justification by Faith

Robert L. Reymond

THE CURRENT controversy between the traditional Reformation position, on the one hand, and the "Shepherd" position, on the other, over the Pauline doctrine of justification by faith has a history. Evangelicals were confronted in the 1970s by several forks in the road where they chose the wrong road because their guides were highly respected theologians. The "Shepherd fork" that asks evangelicals to opt for justification both by a living faith in Christ and by the works this living faith produces came in the early to mid-70s and has continued to plague the church to this day. The next significant fork on this wrong road where many evangelicals took a second wrong road was at the "Sanders/Dunn fork" in the late 70s and early 80s.[1] Now it is a truism that when one loses his way he should retrace his steps if he can, locate the fork (or forks) where he chose the wrong road, and take the other road. In order to assist evangelicals to retrace their steps, since

---

1. See E. P. Sanders, *Paul and Palestinian Judaism, A Comparison of Patterns of Religion* (Fortress, 1977), and James D. G. Dunn, "The New Perspective on Paul" in *Bulletin of the John Rylands University Library of Manchester* 65 (1983), 95-122.

O. Palmer Robertson has addressed the "Shepherd fork,"[2] I propose in this essay to address the second fork in the road, the "Sanders/Dunn fork."

The Most Debated Topic among Paul Scholars Today

The most debated topic among Paul scholars today is Paul's understanding of the law and more specifically the meaning of his key phrase, "works of law" (ἔργα νόμου, *erga nomou*).[3] By this phrase he summarily characterized what he was so strongly setting off over against his own doctrine of justification by faith in Jesus Christ, namely, justification by "works of

2. See O. Palmer Robertson, *The Current Justification Controversy*. The Trinity Foundation, 2003.

3. Paul used the phrase, "works of law," eight times in his writings: he affirmed that no one can be justified by "works of law" (*Galatians* 2:16 [3 times]; *Romans* 3:20, 28), that the Spirit is not received by "works of law" (*Galatians* 3:2, 5), and that all those whose religious efforts are characterized by "works of law" are under the law's curse (*Galatians* 3:10). Also the simple ἔργα, *erga*, in *Romans* 4:2, 6; 9:12, 32; 11:6; and *Ephesians* 2:9 almost certainly has the same meaning, thereby bringing the total number of texts in which Paul alluded to the concept to fourteen. I would argue that Paul intended by this phrase "things done in accordance with *whatever* the law commands – the moral law no less than the ritual, the ritual laws no less than the moral," with the intention of achieving right standing before God.

Although C. E. B. Cranfield argued in his essay, "St. Paul and the Law," in the *Scottish Journal of Theology* 17 (1964), 43-68, that Paul coined this Greek phrase because no designation was available in Greek to represent the idea of "legalism," close equivalents have been found in the Qumran material, for example, מעשי תורה, *m'sy thôrāh* ("works of law") in *4QFlor* 1.1-7 (= *4Q174*); מעשי בתורה, *m'sy bhthôrāh* ("works in the law") in *1QS* 5:20-24; 6:18; and מקצת מעשי התורה, *mqtsth m'sy hthôrāh* ("some of the works of the law") in *4QMMT* 3:29, all which seem to denote the works that the Qumran Community thought the law required of it in order to maintain its separate communal existence.

law." Obviously we will not be able fully to comprehend the precise nature of the doctrine Paul wanted to put in its place if we do not grasp the precise nature of the teaching he so vigorously opposed. This debate is raging today between Protestant Pauline scholars, particularly German Lutheran scholars and historic Reformed theologians, on the one hand, and the "new perspective" views of E. P. Sanders, James D. G. Dunn and their followers, on the other. The former view – the "traditional Reformation view" – contends that Jews in general in Paul's day and the Pharisees in particular were obeying the law to accumulate merit before God for themselves and thereby to earn salvation, and that this is the reason Paul appears at times to inveigh against the law: His kinsmen according to the flesh or at least a large portion of first-century world Jewry (not all Jews, of course, since there was always "a remnant chosen by grace," *Romans* 11:5) had come to view the law *legalistically* as the instrument for the acquisition of righteousness. C. E. B. Cranfield has argued that Paul's criticism of the law was a criticism of its then-current *perversion* into the legalism of works-righteousness; it is thus the "legalistic misunderstanding and perversion of the law," not the law itself, which kills.[4]

---

4. C. E. B. Cranfield, "St. Paul and the Law," 43-68; see also his response to his critics, "'The Works of the Law' in the Epistle to the Romans" in *Journal for the Study of the New Testament* 43 (1991), 89-101. Of course, Paul's criticism of "covenantal legalism" was not an innovation: Both the Old Testament prophets, by their denunciation of a preoccupation with the niceties of sacrificial ritual while obedience from the heart expressed in humility, compassion, and justice for the oppressed was non-existent (*1 Samuel* 15:22-23; *Psalms* 40:6-8; 51:16-17; *Isaiah* 1:10-20; *Amos* 2:6-8; 4:4-5; 5:21-24; *Micah* 6:6-8), and later Jesus himself, by his denunciation of the

Sanders' "Covenantal Nomism"

The traditional Protestant view had not gone unchallenged, of course. For example, in 1894 C. G. Montefiore, a distinguished Jewish scholar, had argued that the rabbinic literature of the time speaks of a compassionate and forgiving God and of rabbis whose daily prayer was "Sovereign of all worlds! Not because of our righteous acts do we lay our supplications before you, but because of your abundant mercies" (*b. Yoma* 87b).[5] And in 1927 G. F. Moore had urged in his *Judaism in the First Centuries of the Christian Era*[6] that the earliest literature of rabbinic religion spoke constantly of grace, forgiveness, and repentance. But New Testament theologians had

---

concern of the hypocritical scribes and Pharisees for their external, presumably merit-aquiring observance of the law while their hearts were far from the Lord (*Matthew* 5:21-6:18; 23:1-39; *Mark* 7:1-13; *Luke* 11:37-54), had spoken against such a perversion of the law's purpose.

So also Ridderbos ("Section 21: The Antithesis with Judaism" in *Paul: An Outline of His Theology*, 130-135), 132-134, who insists that for the Judaism of Paul's day "the law is the unique means to acquire for oneself merit, reward, righteousness before God, and the instrument given by God to subjugate the evil impulse and to lead the good to victory...for the Jews the law was the pre-eminent means of salvation, indeed the real 'substance of life'.... Judaism knew no other way of salvation than that of the law, and...it saw even the mercy and the forgiving love of God as lying precisely in the fact that they enable the sinner once more to build for his eternal future on the ground of the law.... It is this redemptive significance that Judaism ascribed to the law against which the antithesis in Paul's doctrine of sin is directed."

5. C. G. Montefiore, "First Impressions of Paul," *Jewish Quarterly Review* 6 (1894), 428-475; "Rabbinic Judaism and the Epistles of St. Paul," *Jewish Quarterly Review* 13 (1900-1901), 161-217.

6. G. F. Moore, *Judaism in the First Centuries of the Christian Era: The Age of the Tannaim* (2 volumes; Harvard University, 1927).

largely ignored the implications of such studies. The publication of E. P. Sanders' programmatic *Paul and Palestinian Judaism*[7] in 1977, however, brought a "rude awakening" to what Dunn calls the "quiet cul-de-sac" that the field of New Testament study had become, making it necessary for anyone earnestly desiring to understand Christian beginnings in general or Pauline theology in particular to reconsider the traditional Protestant view.[8]

Sanders, in the name of what he terms "covenantal nomism," challenged the traditional view as being simply a myth. He argues, first, that traditional Protestantism, particularly Lutheranism, has been guilty of reading back into New Testament times *late* Jewish sources (such as those from the fifth century A.D. that picture the final judgment as a

7. E. P. Sanders, *Paul and Palestinian Judaism, A Comparison of Patterns of Religion* (Fortress, 1977); see also his more important *Paul, the Law, and the Jewish People* (Fortress, 1983), his *Paul* (Oxford University Press, 1991), and his *Judaism: Practice and Belief, 63 B.C.E. – 66 C.E.* (SCM, 1992), all four works unified by their common conviction concerning the *non-legalistic* nature of first-century Palestinian Judaism and their corresponding rejection of the traditional Lutheran Reformation understanding of the law/gospel antithesis as the key to Paul's view of the law and the theology of his Jewish opposition. See also W. D. Davies, *Paul and Rabbinic Judaism: Some Rabbinic Elements in Pauline Theology* (1948; fourth edition; Fortress, 1980), who argues that Paul's doctrine of justification by faith apart from "works of law" was only one metaphor among many of the time (221-223) and that Paul was simply a Pharisee for whom the messianic age had dawned (71-73).

8. The reason Sanders' effort was heard while the previous efforts were largely ignored is traceable to the new historical situation and social climate which obtained at the time as the result of, first, the Nazi Holocaust in the aftermath of which the traditional denigration of Judaism as the negative side of the debate with the Protestant doctrine of justification could no longer be stomached, and second, Vatican II which absolved the Jewish people of deicide.

matter of weighing up merits and demerits) and thereby inappropriately construing the conflict between Paul and his Jewish opponents in terms of debates that occurred at the time of the magisterial Reformation between Luther and Rome; and second, that conversely first-century Palestinian Judaism had not been seduced by merit theology into becoming a religion of legalistic works-righteousness wherein right standing before God was earned by good works in a system of strict justice. He contends rather (1) that the covenant, the law, and the Jews' special status as the elect people of God were all gifts of God's grace to Israel; (2) that the Jews did not have to earn – and knowing this were not trying to earn – what they already had received by grace; (3) that Judaism did not teach that "works of law" were the condition for entry into the covenant but only for continuing in and maintaining covenant status (that is to say, that salvation comes not from meritorious works but through belonging to the covenant people of God),[9] which "pattern of religion," Sanders contends (I think wrongly), is also found in Paul; and (4) that the only real bone of contention between an (at times) incoherent and inconsistent Paul (who was not unwilling to distort his opponents' positions at times in order to safeguard his own) and his Jewish contemporaries was not soteriology (what one must do in order to be saved) but purely and simply *Christology* (what one should think about Christ). Which is just to say that Paul saw Christianity as superior to Judaism only because while the Jews thought they had in the covenant a *national* charter of privilege, Paul viewed covenantal privilege as *open to all* who have faith in Christ and who accordingly stand in conti-

9. Sanders, *Paul and Palestinian Judaism*, 422.

nuity with Abraham. Or to put it more simply, Paul viewed Christianity as superior to Judaism only because Judaism was not Christianity.

It is indeed true, as Sanders demonstrates from his in-depth examination of the Qumran literature, the Apocryphal literature, the Pseudepigraphal literature, and the rabbinic literature of the first two-hundred years after Christ, that one can find many references in this material to God's election of Israel and to his grace and mercy toward the nation. And, of course, if Sanders is right about the non-legalistic nature of Palestinian Judaism in Paul's day, then Douglas J. Moo is correct when he asserts that the traditional Reformation view of Paul's polemic "is left hanging in mid-air, and it is necessary either to accuse Paul of misunderstanding (or misinterpreting) his opponents, or to find new opponents for him to be criticizing."[10] Regarding the first of these possibilities, I can only say that the modern scholar, whether Christian or Jew, who supposes that he understands better or interprets more accurately first-century Palestinian Judaism than Paul did, is a rash person indeed! Moreover, Sanders makes too much of his, in my opinion, methodologically flawed findings on the "non-legalistic" character of first-century Palestinian Judaism, since first-century Palestinian Judaism, as he himself recognizes, also taught that the elect man was obligated, even though

10. Douglas J. Moo, "Paul and the Law in the Last Ten Years" in *Scottish Journal of Theology* 40 (1987), 293. See also Moo's "'Law,' 'Works of the Law,' and Legalism in Paul," *Westminster Theological Journal* 45 (1983), 73-100; and his *The Epistle to the Romans* (Eerdmans, 1996), particularly his comments on *Romans* 3:20 and the following "Excursus: Paul, 'Works of the Law,' and First-Century Judaism" (206-217), that take these developments into account, and Mark A. Seifrid, "Blind Alleys in the Controversy over the Paul of History" in *Tyndale Bulletin* 45.1 (1994), 73-95.

he would do so imperfectly (for which imperfections the law's sacrificial system provided the remedy), to obey the law in order to *maintain* his covenant status and to *remain* in the covenant. But this is to acknowledge, as Moo notes, that

> even in Sanders's proposal, works play such a prominent role that it is fair to speak of a "synergism" of faith and works that elevates works to a crucial salvific role. For, while works, according to Sanders, are not the means of "getting in," they are essential to "staying in." When, then, we consider the matter from the perspective of the final judgment – which we must in Jewish theology – it is clear that "works," even in Sanders's view, play a necessary and instrumental role in "salvation."[11]

---

11. Moo, *The Epistle to the Romans*, 215. In his somewhat dated but nonetheless very insightful *Biblical Theology* (Eerdmans, 1948), Geerhardus Vos also affirms that Judaism contained a large strain of legalism, stating that the Judaic "philosophy asserted that the law was intended, on the principle of meritoriousness, to enable Israel to earn the blessedness of the world to come" (142). He then explains why and how the Judaizers went wrong:

"It is true, certain of the statements of the Pentateuch and of the O. T. in general may on the surface seem to favor the Judaistic position. That the law cannot be kept is nowhere stated in so many words. And not only this, that the keeping of the law will be rewarded, is stated once and again. Israel's retention of the privileges of the *berith* [covenant] is made dependent on obedience. It is promised that he who shall do the commandments shall find life through them. Consequently, writers have not been lacking, who declared, that, from a historical point of view, their sympathies went with the Judaizers, and not with Paul. Only a moment's reflection is necessary to prove that...precisely from a broad historical standpoint Paul had far more accurately grasped the purport of the law than his opponents. The law was given after the redemption from Egypt had been accomplished, and the people had already entered upon the enjoyment of many of the blessings of the *berith*. Particularly, their taking pos-

Moo goes on to note in the same connection:

> ...there is reason to conclude that Judaism was more "le-
> galistic" than Sanders thinks. In passage after passage in
> his scrutiny of the Jewish literature, he dismisses a "le-
> galistic" interpretation by arguing that the covenantal
> framework must be read into the text or that the passage
> is homiletical rather than theological in intent. But was
> the covenant as pervasive as Sanders thinks? Might not
> lack of reference in many Jewish works imply that it had

---

session of the promised land could not have been made dependent on previous observance of the law, for during their journey in the wilderness many of its prescripts could not be observed. It is plain, then, that law-keeping did not figure at that juncture as the meritorious ground of life-inheritance. The latter is based on grace alone, no less emphatically than Paul himself places salvation on that ground. But, while this is so, it might still be objected, that law-observance, if not the ground of receiving, is yet made the ground for retention of the privileges inherited. Here it can not, of course, be denied that a real connection exists. But the Judaizers went wrong in inferring that the connection must be *meritorious*, that, if Israel keeps the cherished gifts of Jehovah through observance of His law, this must be so, because in strict justice they had *earned* them. The connection is of a totally different kind. It belongs not to the legal sphere of merit, but to the symbolico-typical sphere of *appropriateness of expression*. ...the abode of Israel in Canaan typified the heavenly, perfected state of God's people. Under these circumstances the ideal of absolute conformity to God's law of legal holiness had to be upheld. Even though they were not able to keep this law in the Pauline, spiritual sense, yea, even though they were unable to keep it externally and ritually, the requirement could not be lowered. When apostasy on a general scale took place, they could not remain in the promised land. When they disqualified themselves for typifying the state of holiness, they *ipso facto* disqualified themselves for typifying that of blessedness, and had to go into captivity.... And in Paul's teaching the strand that corresponds to this Old Testament doctrine of holiness as the indispensable (though not meritorious) condition of receiving the inheritance is still distinctly traceable" (142-144).

been lost sight of in a more general reliance on Jewish identity? And does not theology come into expression in homiletics? Indeed, is it not in more practically oriented texts that we discover what people *really* believe? Sanders may be guilty of underplaying a drift toward a more legalistic posture in first-century Judaism. We must also reckon with the possibility that many "lay" Jews were more legalistic than the surviving literary remains of Judaism would suggest. Certainly the undeniable importance of the law in Judaism would naturally open the way to viewing doing the law in itself as salvific. The gap between the average believer's theological views and the informed views of religious leaders is often a wide one. If Christianity has been far from immune to legalism, is it likely to think that Judaism, at any state of its development, was?[12]

12. Moo, *The Epistle to the Romans*, 216-217. While I disagree with Jacob Neusner's final conclusion, see also his *Rabbinic Judaism: Structure and System* (Fortress, 1995), 7-13, 20-23, wherein he heaps scorn upon Sanders' literary efforts, not so much for his conclusions but because he tends by his method to join all Judaic religious systems into a single, harmonious "Judaism." While Neusner appreciates the methodology of Sanders' *Paul and Palestinian Judaism* much more than the methodology and conclusions reflected in his *Judaism: Practice and Belief 63 B.C.E. – 66 C.E.*, he still faults Sanders' earlier handling of the Mishna and the other rabbinic sources because, says Neusner, the Pauline-Lutheran questions he brings to it are simply not these sources' central concerns: "Sanders's earlier work is profoundly flawed by the category formation that he imposes on his sources; that distorts and misrepresents the Judaic system of these sources" (22). He explains:

"Sanders quotes all documents equally with no effort at differentiation among them. He seems to have culled sayings from the diverse sources he has chosen and written them down on cards, which he proceeded to organize around his critical categories. Then he has constructed his paragraphs and sections by flipping through these cards and commenting on this and

In support of Moo's contentions one could cite, as samplings of Judaic thought in this regard, *Sirach* (also known as *Ecclesiasticus*) 3:3, 14-15, 30-31, a second-century B.C. Jewish writing, that teaches quite clearly that human good deeds atone for sins:

> 3 Whoever honors his father atones for sins,...
> 14 For kindness to a father will not be forgotten,
>   and against your sins it will be credited to you;
> 15 In the day of your affliction it will be remembered in your favor,
>   as frost in fair weather, your sins will melt away....
> 30 Water extinguishes a blazing fire:
>   so almsgiving atones for sin.

---

that. So there is no context in which a given saying is important in its own setting, in its own document. This is Billerbeck scholarship.

"The diverse rabbinic documents require study in and on their own terms... [But Sanders'] claim to have presented an account of 'the Rabbis' and their opinions is not demonstrated and not even very well argued. We hardly need to dwell on the still more telling fact that Sanders has not shown how systemic comparison is possible when, in point of fact, the issues of one document, or of one system of which a document is a part, are simply not the same as the issues of some other document or system; he is oblivious to all documentary variations and differences of opinion. That is, while he has succeeded in finding rabbinic sayings on topics of central importance to Paul (or Pauline theology), he has ignored the context and authentic character of the setting in which he has found these sayings. He lacks all sense of proportion and coherence, because he has not even asked whether these sayings form the center and core of the rabbinic system or even of a given rabbinic document. To state matters simply, how do we know that 'the Rabbis' and Paul are talking about the same thing, so that we can compare what they have to say? If it should turn out that 'the Rabbis' and Paul are not talking about the same thing, then what is it that we have to compare? I think, nothing at all" (22-23).

[31] Whoever requites favors gives thought to the future;
at the moment of his falling he will find support.
(See also *Sirach* 29:11-13 and *Tobit* 4:7-11.)

Sanders also ignores Flavius Josephus' frequent insistence that God's grace is meted out in response to merit,[13] and he simply discounts the argument of 2 *Esdras*[14] as an atypical exception here.[15] And Qumran document *1QS* 11:2, 3 states: "For I belong to the God of my vindication and the perfection of my way is in his hand with the virtue of my heart. And *with*

13. In his *Against Apion*, II, 217b-218, for example, Josephus writes: "For those...who live *in accordance with our laws* [νομίμως, *nomimōs*] the prize is not silver or gold, no crown of wild olive or of parsley with any such public mark of distinction. No; each individual, relying on the witness of his own conscience and the lawgiver's prophecy, confirmed by the sure testimony of God, is firmly persuaded that *to those who observe the laws* [τοῖς τοὺς νόμους διαφυλάξασι, *tois tous nomous diaphulaxasi*] and, if they must needs die for them, willingly meet death, God has granted *a renewed existence* [γενέσθαι πάλιν, *genesthai palin*] and in the revolution of the ages the gift of *a better life* [βίον ἀμείνω, *bion ameinō*]."

In his *Discourse to the Greeks on Hades* Josephus states that "to those that have done well [God will give] an everlasting fruition," and more specifically that "the just shall remember only their righteous actions, whereby they have attained the heavenly kingdom."

14. 2 *Esdras* is 4 *Esdras* in the appendix of the Roman Catholic *Vulgate* Bible, with chapters 3-14 being a late first-century A.D. work written by an unknown Palestinian Jew in response to the destruction of Jerusalem in A.D. 70.

15. See, for example, the following statements in 2 *Esdras*:
7:77: "For you have a treasure of works laid up with the Most High."
7:78-94: "Now, concerning death, the teaching is: When the decisive decree has gone forth from the Most High that a man shall die...if [the spirits are] those...who have despised his law...such spirits shall not enter into habitations, but shall immediately wander about in torments, ever grieving and sad...because they scorned the law of the Most High.... Now this is the order of those who have kept the ways of the Most High, when

my righteous deeds he will wipe away my transgressions."[16] *1QS* 3:6-8; 8:6-10; 9:4 also attribute an atoning efficacy to the Qumran Community's deeds. Turning to the New Testament, one may also cite here the opinion of the "believers who belonged to the party of the Pharisees" (*Acts* 15:5) who declared: "Unless you [Gentiles] are circumcised, according to the custom taught by Moses, you cannot be saved" (*Acts* 15:1). I grant that the focus of these *Acts* verses is directed toward what the Pharisee party in the church thought Gentiles had to do in order to be saved, but it is surely appropriate to conclude, first, that they would have believed that they themselves had to do the same thing in order to be saved, and second, that they were

---

they shall be separated from their mortal bodies. During the time that they lived in it, they...withstood danger every hour, that they might keep the law of the Lawgiver perfectly. Therefore...they shall see with great joy the glory of him who receives them...because...while they were alive they kept the law which was given them in trust."

7:105: "...no one shall ever pray for another on that day...for then every one shall bear his own righteousness or unrighteousness."

7:133: "[The Most High] is gracious to those who turn in repentance to his law."

8:33: "For the righteous, who have many works laid up with thee, shall receive their reward in consequence of their own deeds."

8:55-56: "Therefore do not ask anymore questions about the multitude of those who perish. For they also received freedom, but they despised the Most High, and were contemptuous of his law."

9:7-12: "And it shall be that every one who will be saved and will be able to escape on account of his works...will see my salvation in my land...and as many as scorned my law while they still had freedom...these must in torment acknowledge it after death."

See also B. W. Longenecker, *2 Esdras* (Sheffield Academic, 1995).

16. For the defense of "with my righteous deeds" and not "and in his righteousness" as the more likely original reading see Mark A. Seifrid, "Blind Alleys," 81-82, fn. 28.

apparently reflecting what at least the Pharisees – the strictest sect of Judaism – would also have believed.

Moreover, in Paul's "allegory" in *Galatians* 4:21-31, wherein he first declares that "Hagar stands for Mount Sinai in Arabia and corresponds to *the present city of Jerusalem* [literally "the now Jerusalem," τῇ νῦν 'Ιερουσαλήμ, *tē nun Ierousalēm*], because she is in slavery with her children," thereby placing "the now Jerusalem," which stands within his "Hagar-Sinai-law-bondage" matrix, in bondage to the law (4:25), and then contrasts "the now Jerusalem" with "the Jerusalem that is above [literally "the above Jerusalem," ἡ ἄνω 'Ιερουσαλήμ, *hē anō Ierousalēm*]" that is "free" and the Christian's "mother," it is apparent that Paul's expression, "the now Jerusalem," goes beyond the Judaizers who were troubling his churches and, in the words of Ronald Fung, "stands by metonymy for Judaism, with its trust in physical descent from Abraham and reliance on legal observance as the way of salvation."[17] In sum, Paul by this allegory is saying that the nation of Israel, because of its unbelief and bondage to the law, is in actually a nation of spiritual Ishmaelites, sons of the bondwoman Hagar, and not true Israelites at all!

Finally, if the foregoing data are not sufficient to show Sanders' error, and if one is willing as I am to give Paul his rightful due as an inspired apostle of Christ, then as the *coup de grâce* to Sanders' "new perspective" on first-century Palestinian Ju-

---

17. Ronald Y. K. Fung, *The Epistle to the Galatians* (NICNT; Eerdmans, 1988), 209; see also C. K. Barrett, "The Allegory of Abraham, Sarah, and Hagar in the Argument of Galatians" in *Rechtfertigung, Festschrift für Ernst Käsemann*, edited by Johannes Friedrich, Wolfgang Pöhlmann, and Peter Stuhlmacher (Göttingen: Vandenhoeck & Ruprecht, 1976); republished in *Essays on Paul*, 154-170.

daism, Paul writes in *Romans* 9:30-32, 10:2-4:

> When then shall we say? That the Gentiles, who did not pursue righteousness, have obtained it, a righteousness that is by faith; but Israel, *who pursued law [as a means to] righteousness,*[18] did not attain [the requirements of that] law. Why not? Because *they pursued it not by faith but as if it were by works* [of law[19]].... For I can testify about [the Israelites] that they are zealous for God, but their zeal is not based on knowledge. Since they did not know the righteousness that comes from God and *sought to establish their own,* they did not submit to God's righteousness. Christ is the end of "law-keeping" [literally "law"] as a means to [εἰς, *eis*[20]] righteousness to all who believe[21] [emphasis supplied].

18. I construe δικαιοσύνης, *dikaiosunēs*, to be an ablative of means. Moo virtually says this when he concludes his discussion of the phrase νόμον δικαιοσύνης, *nomon dikaiosunēs*, here by saying: "'Law,' therefore, remains the topic of Paul's teaching throughout this verse and a half [*Romans* 9:31-32a], but law conceived as a means to righteousness" (625-626).

19. I have added this prepositional phrase only to bring out what I think is Paul's intended meaning and not because I think that it reflects the originality of the textual variant ἔργων νόμου, *ergōn nomou*, supported by א2, D, K, P, Y 33, 81, 104 etc., a few church fathers, and a few versions.

20. By construing the εἰς, *eis*, here as denoting "means," I have conformed Paul's statement here with his earlier phrase, "law [as a means to] righteousness," in 9:31.

21. C. K. Barrett, in "Romans 9:30-10:21: Fall and Responsibility of Israel" in *Essays on Paul,* correctly explains Paul's intention in these verses this way: "...the only way to achieve righteousness (which is what the righteous law requires) is by faith. This way the Gentiles, who really had no choice in the matter, had adopted, when they were surprised by the gospel.... Israel had not done this. They had been given the law...and had sought to do what they understood it to mean; but *they had misunderstood their own law, thinking that it was to be obeyed on the principle of works,* whereas it demanded obedience rendered in, consisting of, faith" (141, emphasis supplied).

In sum, while both Judaism and Paul viewed obedience to the law as having an appropriate place in the covenant way of life, there was this difference: whereas Paul viewed the Christian's obedience as (at best) the *fruit* and *evidentiary sign* of the fact that one is a member of the covenant community, Judaism saw obedience to the law as the *instrumental basis* for continuing in salvation through the covenant. Thus the legalistic principle – even though it occurred within the context of the covenant as a kind of "covenantal legalism" – was still present and ultimately that principle came to govern the soteric status of the individual. This is just to say that Second Temple Judaism apparently over time became focused more and more on an "instrumental nomism" and less and less on a "gracious covenantalism of faith." Paul rightly saw that *any* obligation to accomplish a works-righteousness to *any* degree on the sinner's part would negate the principle of *sola gratia* altogether (*Romans* 11:5-6), obligate him to obey the whole law (*Galatians* 3:10; 5:3), and make the cross-work of Christ of no value to him (*Galatians* 2:21; 5:2).[22] Finally, Paul does not represent Christianity as superior to Judaism only because of a kind of dispensational shift within salvation history from Judaism to Christianity. His differences with Judaism were far more radical and passionate than that.

---

22. For a detailed critical analysis of Sanders' thesis, see M. A. Seifrid, *Justification by Faith: The Origin and Development of a Central Pauline Theme* (*NovTSup* 68; Brill, 1992); S. Westerholm, *Israel's Law and the Church's Faith: Paul and His Recent Interpreters* (Eerdmans, 1988); C. G. Kruse, *Paul, the Law and Justification* (InterVarsity, 1996); and Karl T. Cooper, "Paul and Rabbinic Soteriology" in *Westminster Theological Journal* 44 (1982), 123-139.

Dunn's "New Perspective"

James D. G. Dunn, who accepts, not without some reserva-
tions, Sanders' understanding of first-century Palestinian Judaism, in his *Jesus, Paul and the Law*[23] urges that Paul's "works
of law" phrase does not refer to works done to achieve righteousness, that is, to legalism, but to the Mosaic law particularly as that law came to focus for Israel in the observance of
such Jewish "identity markers" as circumcision, food laws, and
Sabbath-keeping. That is to say, Paul's "works of law" phrase
refers to a subset of the law's commands, encapsulating *Jewish*
existence in the nation's covenant relationship with God or, to
quote Dunn himself, "the self-understanding and obligation
accepted by practicing Jews that E. P. Sanders encapsulated
quite effectively in the phrase 'covenantal nomism.'"[24] In sum,

23. James D. G. Dunn, *Jesus, Paul and the Law: Studies in Mark and
Galatians* (Westminster/John Knox, 1990), 183-206, 215-236; see also his
"The New Perspective on Paul" in *Bulletin of the John Rylands University
Library of Manchester* 65 (1983), 95-122. Moo, *The Epistle to the Romans*,
provides the "Dunn bibliography" on the issue (207, fn. 57), to which must
be added his *The Theology of Paul the Apostle* (Eerdmans, 1998), 334-371.

24. In his essay, "Echoes of Intra-Jewish Polemic in Paul's Letter to the
Galatians" in *Journal of Biblical Literature* 112 (1993), Dunn states that the
phrase refers to "acts of obedience required by the law of all faithful Jews,
all members of the people with whom God had made the covenant at
Sinai – the self-understanding and obligation accepted by practicing Jews
that E. P. Sanders encapsulated quite effectively in the phrase 'covenantal
nomism'" (466). In his more recent *The Theology of Paul the Apostle* Dunn
declares quite forcefully: "I do not (and never did!) claim that 'works of
the law' denote only circumcision, food laws, and Sabbath. A careful reading of my 'New Perspective' should have made it clear that, as in Galatians
2, these were particular focal or crisis points for (and demonstrations of)
a generally nomistic attitude" (358, fn 97, emphasis supplied). If this is
actually the case, then Dunn is saying that first-century Jewry held gen-

for Dunn the heart issue for Paul was the inclusion of Gentile Christians in the messianic community on an equal footing with Jewish Christians. In other words, for Paul his bone of contention with Judaism was not so much with an imagined attempt to acquire a merit-based righteousness before God as much as it was with Israel's *prideful* insistence on its covenantal racial exclusiveness: Israel shut Gentiles out of the people of God because they did not observe *their* ethno-social "identity markers." And apparently many Jewish Christians wanted Gentile Christians to observe these Jewish "identity markers" before they would or could share table fellowship with them (see *Acts* 10:28; *Galatians* 2:11-13). Paul by his "works of law" phrase was opposing then the Old Testament *ritual* laws that kept Israel in its national identity (see *Numbers* 23:9) apart from Gentiles.

Whereas Sanders' conclusions, in my opinion, go too far, Dunn's interpretation of Paul's concern, in my opinion, is reductionistic and does not go far enough. Paul was indeed concerned with – and vigorously opposed – the spirit of racial exclusiveness within Messiah's community, but this does not appear to be his concern in his sermon in the synagogue at Pisidian Antioch when he declared that "through [Jesus] *everyone who believes* [πᾶς ὁ πιστεύων, *pas ho pisteuōn*] *is justified* [δικαιοῦται, *dikaioutai*] *from all things* [ἀπὸ πάντων, *apo pantōn*], from which you could not be justified by [keeping] the [whole] law of Moses" (*Acts* 13:39). Nor does he hesitate to relate his "works of law" terminology universally to "no flesh" (literally "not...all flesh," οὐ...πᾶσα σάρξ, *ou...pasa sarx*] in

---

erally to a legalistic view of salvation and his "New Perspective" is not really new.

Romans 3:20,[25] which surely includes both Gentiles (see *Romans* 3:9) who obviously *were not obligated to observe Israel's circumcision or food laws* but who, according to Paul, were nonetheless regarded by God as transgressors of his law (see *Romans* 1:18-32) and the people of Israel who *were obligated to observe and who were in fact observing their national identity markers* (see *Romans* 2:25-29), but who also, according to Paul, were still regarded by God as transgressors of his law (see *Romans* 2:21-24), both accordingly standing under the law's condemnation.[26] Which is just to say that Paul's "works of law" phrase in *Romans* 3:20 intended more than simply observance (or in the case of Gentiles, non-observance) of Israel's national identity markers. *The phrase included observance of God's moral law, too.* But if the phrase in 3:20 includes observance of the moral law of God as well, it surely means the same in 3:28 where Paul declares: "For we maintain that a man [*any* man; see 3:29-30] is justified by faith apart from [legalistic] works of law." And immediately after he establishes mankind's guilt before God in terms of the inability of the "works of law" to justify anyone (3:20) Paul places those "works of law" as the false way to righteousness over against and in contrast to faith in Christ's saving work as the one true

25. Note too his universalistic phrases, "every mouth" (πᾶν στόμα, *pan stoma*) and "the whole world" (πᾶς ὁ κόσμος, *pas ho kosmos*) in *Romans* 3:19.

26. Moo, *The Epistle to the Romans*, writes: "The 'works' mentioned [in *Romans* 3:20] must...be the 'works' Paul has spoken of in chap. 2. But it is not circumcision – let alone other 'identity markers' that are not even mentioned in Rom. 1-3 – that the Jew 'does' in Rom. 2; it is, generally, what is demanded by the law, the 'precepts' (v. 26; cf. vv. 22-23, 25, 27). Therefore, 3:20 must deny not the adequacy of Jewish *identity* to justify, but the adequacy of Jewish *works* to justify" (214).

way to righteousness (see *Romans* 3:21-25: δικαιοσύνη θεοῦ διὰ πίστεως Ἰησοῦ Χριστοῦ, *dikaiosunē theou dia pisteōs Iēsou Christou*). Then when one takes into account Paul's reference to *human* "boasting" both in 3:27 (καύχησις, *kauchēsis*) and 4:2 (καύχημα, *kauchēma*) and his insistence in *Romans* 4 that Abraham was not justified by his "works" (ἐξ ἔργων, *ex ergōn*, 4:2) or by his "working" (ἐργαζομένῳ, *ergazomenō*, 4:4-5) – which words, given their proximity to *Romans* 3:20 and 3:28, are almost certainly his theological shorthand for his earlier "works of law" expression – it should be again apparent that Paul's "works of law" phrase intends more than the observance (or in the case of Gentiles, non-observance) of certain Jewish identity markers *since Abraham lived before the giving of the ritual law of the Mosaic Law to Israel.*[27]

Then to Peter who, after enjoying table fellowship with Gentiles for a time at Antioch, succumbed to the pressures of the Judaizers Paul said:

> We [apostles] who are Jews by birth and not "Gentile sinners" know that a man is not justified *by observing the law* [ἐξ ἔργων νόμου, *ex ergōn nomou*], but by faith in Jesus Christ. So we, too, have put our faith in Christ Jesus that we may be justified by faith in Christ and not *by observing the law* [ἐξ ἔργων νόμου, *ex ergōn nomou*], because *by observing the law* [ἐξ ἔργων νόμου, *ex ergōn nomou*] *no one* [note again the universality in οὐ...πᾶσα σάρξ, *ou...pasa sarx*, "not...all flesh"] will be justified [*Galatians* 2:15-16].

27. W. Gutbrod, νόμος, *nomos* (and the νομ-, *nom-*, word cluster), *Theological Dictionary of the New Testament*, translated by Geoffrey W. Bromiley (Eerdmans, 1967), IV:1072, also declares that Paul "works out his position" in regard to the law "primarily with ref. to the ethical commandments, esp. those of the Decalogue which apply to all men."

Then, after asking the "Judaized" Gentile Christians of Galatia the twin questions: "Did you receive the Spirit *by observing the law* [ἐξ ἔργων νόμου, *ex ergōn nomou*], or *by believing what you heard* [ἐξ ἀκοῆς πίστεως, *ex akoēs pisteōs*]" (*Galatians* 3:2), and "Does God give you his Spirit and work miracles among you because you *observe the law* [ἐξ ἔργων νόμου, *ex ergōn nomou*] or because you *believe what you heard* [ἐξ ἀκοῆς πίστεως, *ex akoēs pisteōs*]" (*Galatians* 3:5), he declares:

> *All who* [ὅσοι, *hosoi*, "As many as"] *rely on observing the law* [ἐξ ἔργων νόμου εἰσίν, *ex ergōn nomou eisin*] are under a curse, for it is written: "Cursed is *everyone* [πᾶς, *pas*] who does not continue to do *everything* [πᾶσιν, *pasin*] written in the Book of the Law." Clearly *no one* [οὐδεὶς, *oudeis*] is justified before God by the law, because, "The righteous will live by faith" [*Galatians* 3:10-11; see also *Romans* 3:21-28; 4:1-5; *Titus* 3:5].

Who are these people who are "relying on observance of the law" for their salvation? Once again we are struck by Paul's universalistic language. It is true that in his letter to the Romans Paul describes the Jew as one who "*relies* [ἐπαναπαύῃ, *epanapauē*] on the law" (*Romans* 2:17). And it is also true that in the context of the Galatians letter his most immediate opponents are the Judaizers and his Gentile converts who had succumbed to the teaching of the Judaizers. But Paul's "no flesh" (οὐ...πᾶσα σάρξ, *ou...pasa sarx*) expression in *Galatians* 2:16 appears once again to be applicable to anyone and everyone[28] – Jew or Gentile, *the latter of whom had*

28. Observe his universalistic *everyone* [πᾶς, *pas*] and *no one* [οὐδεὶς, *oudeis*] in *Galatians* 2:16.

no obligation to observe circumcision or Israel's food laws – who trusts in his own law-keeping for salvation. And the same must be said for his "as many as" (ὅσοι, *hosoi*), his "everyone" (πᾶς, *pas*) and his "no one" (οὐδείς, *oudeis*) in *Galatians* 3:10-11. Finally, his descriptive *"everything* [πᾶσιν, *pasin*] written in the Book of the Law" in *Galatians* 3:10 suggests once again that he intended by his "works of law" expression not only Israel's identity markers of circumcision, food laws, and Sabbath-keeping, but also the moral law.

Conclusion

It would appear then from these Biblical references, first, that the "new perspective" theologians have not done adequate justice to Paul's teaching when they insist that first-century Palestinian Judaism was *not* a religion of legalistic works-righteousness for it clearly was (as were, of course, the myriad religions of the Gentiles), even though its legalism expressed itself within the context of God's gracious covenant with them in terms of a "maintaining" of covenantal status; second, that by his "works of law" expression Paul intended not just the ceremonial aspects of the law but the whole law in its entirety; and third, that "there is more of Paul in Luther"[29] and the other Reformers with respect to the critical salvific matters that concerned them in the sixteenth century than some of the "new perspective" theologians are inclined to admit.[30]

29. S. Westerholm, *Israel's Law and the Church's Faith: Paul and His Recent Interpreters* (Eerdmans, 1988), 173.

30. One would not be too surprised if Roman Catholic scholars, given their historical opposition to the Reformation interpretation of *Romans*, embraced Sanders' and Dunn's "new perspective," but Joseph A. Fitzmyer in his *Romans: A New Translation with Introduction and Commentary* (An-

In sum, these "new perspective" suggestions that would have Paul saying either more or other than he should have said (Sanders) or less than he actually and clearly intended (Dunn) are "blind alleys" which the church must reject if it hopes to understand Paul's doctrine of justification.[31] And I fervently hope that evangelicals who have taken the influential "Sanders/Dunn fork in the road" will retrace their steps in the light of what I have pointed out in this essay and choose to come down once again on the side of the historic Reformation position on the doctrine of justification by faith alone in the preceptive and penal obedience of Christ alone for their justifying righteousness before God. For Paul insists

1. that there is only one Gospel – justification by faith alone in Christ's righteous obedience and redeeming death alone (*Romans* 1:17; 3:28; 4:5; 10:4; *Galatians* 2:16; 3:10-11, 26; *Philippians* 3:8-9);

2. that any addition to or alteration of the one Gospel is another "gospel" that is not a gospel at all (*Galatians* 1:6-7);

---

chor Bible; Doubleday, 1993), rejects the views of Sanders and Dunn, even arguing that Paul opposes merit theology. B. Byrne, also a Roman Catholic who holds a view of the law that is similar to Fitzmyer's view, like Fitzmyer dismisses the views of Sanders and Dunn in his *Romans* (Collegeville: Glazier, 1996).

31. For readers who are interested in pursuing these topics for themselves, I recommend that they begin with E. Earle Ellis, "Pauline Studies in Recent Research" in *Paul and His Recent Interpreters* (Grand Rapids: Eerdmans, 1961), 11-34; Herman Ridderbos, *Paul: An Outline of His Theology*, translated by John R. De Witt (Grand Rapids: Eerdmans, 1975), 13-43; Scott J. Hafemann, "Paul and His Interpreters," and Thomas R. Schreiner, "Works of the Law," these last two articles appearing in *Dictionary of Paul and His Letters*, 666-679 and 975-979 respectively, and Thomas R. Schreiner, " 'Works of Law' in Paul" in *Novum Testamentum* 33 (1991), 217-244.

3. that those who teach any other "gospel" stand under the anathema of God (*Galatians* 1:8-9); and

4. that those who rely to any degree on their own works or anything in addition to Christ's doing and dying to obtain their salvation nullify the grace of God (*Romans* 11:5-6), make void the cross-work of Christ (*Galatians* 2:21; 5:2), become debtors to keep the entire law (*Galatians* 5:3), and in becoming such "fall from grace" (*Galatians* 5:4), that is, place themselves again under the curse of the law.

Therefore, what one thinks about justification is serious business indeed. The destiny of his own soul depends upon it. Quite correctly did Martin Luther declare Paul's doctrine of justification by faith alone to be the article of the standing or falling church.[32] And John Calvin, declaring it to be "the main hinge upon which religion turns"[33] and "the first and keenest subject of controversy" between Rome and the Reformers of the sixteenth century,[34] stated: "Wherever the knowledge of [justification by faith alone] is taken away, the glory of Christ is extinguished, religion abolished, the Church destroyed, and the hope of salvation utterly overthrown."[35]

32. See Martin Luther's exposition of *Psalm* 130:4 in his *Werke* (Bohlau, 1883 to present), 40.3.352:3.

33. John Calvin, *Institutes of the Christian Religion*, 3.11.1.

34. John Calvin, "Calvin's Reply to Sadoleto," *A Reformation Debate*, edited by John C. Olin (Grand Rapids: Baker, 1976), 66.

35. John Calvin, "Calvin's Reply to Sadoleto," *A Reformation Debate*, 66.

Documents Related to
The Current Justification Controversy

Some Reasons for Dissenting from the Majority Report[1]

Philip E. Hughes

A SITUATION in which I find myself in disagreement with a statement of the Faculty of Westminster Theological Seminary, of all places, on, of all themes, the theme of justification I would have considered unimaginable. That such a situation has now arisen is extremely disconcerting to me personally. The observations that follow are offered in a spirit of Christian charity and good faith, and with the hope that God will graciously bring us in unanimity to a right understanding of the vital Biblical doctrine of justification.

There are, to begin with, two assertions in the Faculty Report to which I wish to draw attention, both because I find them disturbing, and unacceptable, and also because they seem to me to crystallize the issue confronting us: (1) "Faith is never 'faith-in-isolation' (p. 2). and (2) "*Hebrews* 12:14 speaks of 'the holiness without which no one will see the Lord,' which surely involves standing justified before the Lord" (p. 4).

In this discussion it is essential to remember that it is the doctrine of *justification* that is at issue. No one, I imagine,

---

1. The full title is "Some Reasons for Dissenting from the Majority Report of 21 April 1978 on the Subject of JUSTIFICATION Submitted by the Faculty to the Board of Westminster Theological Seminary."

wishes to deny that the faith which is the principle of justification is also the principle of the life of faith, that is, of sanctification, that the root of faith produces the fruit of good works
which are pleasing to God. But the attempt is being made to
connect these good works with faith in such a way that though
defined as non-meritorious they are regarded as necessary to
our future (or final or eschatological) justification: no good
works, no Heaven! This has the effect of calling in question
the perfection and the once-for-all character of the initial –
and, I would insist, the *only* – justification of the sinner who
puts his trust in Christ and to whom the perfect righteousness
of Christ is fully and indefectibly imputed. The righteousness
of Christ which is reckoned to him is the sole ground of his
acceptability before God.

On page 3 of the Faculty Report, endorsement is given to
the concept of justification as a process in three stages: initial
("this initial entry into God's favor"), continuing ("the continued enjoyment of God's favor"), and consummating ("the
consummation of God's favor at the Judgment"). This implies that the sinner's justification is in some real sense dependent on what he does, on the nature of his works, following
his "initial" justification; and this too has the effect of placing
a question-mark over the adequacy of this so-called "initial"
justification: The outcome hangs in suspense until it is seen
whether subsequently the quality of his life is such as to gain
the divine approbation. Only on this basis does it become possible to conceive of justification as continuing and ultimate.

Accordingly, the Report goes on to speak approvingly of
"the 'necessity' of holiness, of good works, for salvation, of the
impossibility of justification without sanctification" (p. 3). Here
sanctification, defined as good works, is added to justification

as requisite for salvation: no good works of sanctification, no salvation! This, I submit, is a serious confusion of the distinctive roles of justification and sanctification. It is the adding of works to faith as necessary for salvation. Biblical support for this position is claimed from *Hebrews* 12:14 which speaks of "the holiness without which no one will see the Lord," and this, the Report affirms, "surely involves standing justified before the Lord" (p. 4). But *our* holiness, our good works performed as Christians, can *never* be even partially a basis for our standing justified before the Lord. As verse 10 of the same chapter shows, the purpose of our discipline as Christians is that we may share *his* holiness; for it is *only* by virtue of our Redeemer's holiness that we can ever hope to stand justified before the Lord. How can it be otherwise when the demand for holiness is absolute (*1 Peter* 1:15f.)? The holiness imputed to the believer at justification is absolute because it is Christ's holiness; and the holiness imparted to the believer at glorification is absolute because then at last, seeing the Saviour as he is, we shall be fully conformed to his likeness (*1 John* 3:2). But in between justification and glorification we are to "strive for...the holiness without which no one will see the Lord": that is to say, we are to be in earnest about advancing in Christ-likeness being progressively conformed to the holiness that is his (*cf. 2 Corinthians* 3:18). *Hebrews* 12:14, in short, is speaking about sanctification, not justification.

The Report advises, however, that not to follow the line it endorses may indicate that one is "inhibited" because one has "isolated faith from good works and encouraged people to think of good works as somehow intrinsically in competition with the unique role of faith" (p. 4). The answer to this is that *where justification is concerned* (and this is the essential qualification) I do indeed isolate faith from good works and I do indeed regard good works as intrinsically in competition with the unique role of faith. I deprecate the extension of justification into the sphere of sanctification, for it is precisely this procedure that leads to the notion that the good works of the Christian have a necessary part to play in his justification.

This means, of course, that I dissent strongly from the earlier assertion that "faith is never faith-in- isolation" (p. 2 of the Report). On the contrary, I maintain that in justification faith is precisely faith-in-isolation. This is the whole point of the Biblical and Reformed emphasis on *faith alone* where our justification is concerned; for justification by faith alone (*sola fide*) means justification by faith in isolation, and particularly in isolation from works. This does not mean, however, that I have any intention of denying the close inter-relationship between faith and works that follows and flows from the believer's justification and should be the hallmark of his life as a Christian, that is, of his sanctification.

Reference is also made in the Faculty Report (p. 3) to the debate that has revolved around the interpretation of the expression "the works of the law" in *Romans* 3 and *Galatians* 3. In these passages Paul declares that "no human being will be justified in God's sight by works of the law" (*Romans* 3:20). and inquires rhetorically: "Did you receive the Spirit by works of the law, or by hearing with faith?" (*Galatians* 3:2). The point is, as all are agreed, that no sinner can be justified by the works of the law (works-righteousness, self-righteousness), but only by faith in Christ, since all are lawbreakers and therefore are condemned, not justified, by the law, as the contexts show. Yet in the case of the Galatian Christians Paul is rebuking them because they are imagining that they can supplement their justification by faith, or improve it, by adding to it works of the law as a further basis of justification. Hence the questions: "Are you so foolish? Having begun with the Spirit, are you now ending with the flesh?" (*Galatians* 3:3).

I am much concerned because it seems to me that the Faculty Report is in effect maintaining a position similar to that which Paul deplored in the Galatian church. I believe that the Apostle's reaction to this Report would have been: "Having begun with faith, are you now ending with works?"

In the discussions leading up to the Report it has been contended that the "works of the law" are, within the context of *Romans* 3 and *Galatians* 3, something quite different from the works of the Christian – that the former are the works of the unbeliever futilely trying to justify himself by works-righteousness, whereas the latter are, by contrast, works that are pleasing and acceptable to God. This understanding is, in general, not a matter of disagreement. But there is more to be said, because the problem with the Galatians was that of a *reversion*, to some degree, to the works of the law as though they were necessary to justification as an adjunct to faith: they were, in fact, turning away from the uniqueness of faith, its aloneness and complete separation from works, in the scheme of our justification before God.

Turning to the *Epistle to the Romans*, one of the numerous texts that have been adduced in support of the contention that there is a "'necessity' of holiness, of good works, for salvation" (p. 4 of the Report again) is *Romans* 2:7, where Paul says: "to those who by patience in well-doing seek for glory and honour and immortality, he will give eternal life." I wish to object that this text is not speaking of the works of the Christian, indeed, that it has nothing to do with justification by faith, or with faith that works and is active. The theme of the immediate context is that of justification by works. Thus in the verse preceding the one quoted Paul asserts that God "will render to every man according to his works" (v. 6) : and in the verses that follow he explains that "there will be tribulation and distress for every human being who does evil,... but glory and honour and peace for every one who does good" (vv. 9, 10). That this is a universal principle is shown by the repeated declaration, "the Jew first and also the Greek."

But this passage must not be separated from the total argument of which it is an important element, for Paul moves on to demonstrate the universality of human sinfulness, insisting that there is absolutely no one at all who does good, and therefore that all without exception are in need of divine grace and of the justification which comes by faith apart from works. "All men, both Jews and Greeks, are under the power of sin," he affirms, and in doing so confirms the teaching of *Psalms* 14 and 53: "None is righteous, no, not one; no one understands, no one seeks for God; all have turned aside, together they have gone wrong; no one does good, not even one" (*Romans* 3:9-12). There is absolutely "no distinction: since all have sinned and fall short of the glory of God" (*Romans* 3:23). And this rules out the possibility of any one in any degree being justified by good works: "no human being will be justified in his sight by works of the law" (*Romans* 3:20). In this way it is shown that, because all have sinned and not even a single one does good, the declaration of *Romans* 2:12, that "all who have sinned without the law (*i.e.*, Gentiles) will also perish without the law, and all who have sinned under the law (*i.e.*, Jews) will be judged by the law," involves the totality of mankind without exception.

Yet the next verse plainly indicates that the law is a principle of justification to the person who keeps it: "it is not the hearers of the law who are righteous before God", Paul states, "but the doers of the law who will be justified" (*Romans* 2:13). The law is essentially a way of life, not an instrument of death. It is precisely God's standard of righteousness, and therefore of justification. Hence the affirmations of the Old Testament that it is by the doing of the law that a man shall live (*Leviticus* 18:5; *Nehemiah* 9:29; *Ezekiel* 20:11, 13). And hence, also, because of the universality of man's law-breaking, the combination with the law of the whole Levitical system of sacrifice and offering for sin.

The same emphasis is evident in the New Testament. In *Luke* 10:25ff., for example, our Lord, in response to the lawyer's question, "Teacher, what shall I do to inherit eternal life?" said: "What is written in the law?" and then, in response to the lawyer's summary of the decalogue, added: "Do this, and you will live!" Likewise, in *Matthew* 19:16ff., on a similar occasion, he tells his interrogator: "If you would enter life, keep the commandments!" So again, in *Galatians* 3, Paul explains that "the law does not rest on faith, for 'He who does them shall live by them'" (*Galatians* 3:12, quoting *Leviticus* 18:5). This is a principle, moreover, to which the Apostle draws attention in the *Epistle to the Romans*. "Moses writes," he says, "that the man who practises the righteousness which is based on the law shall live by it" (*Romans* 10:5). Because, however, of his sinfulness, he found that "the very commandment which promised life proved to be death to me" (*Romans* 7:10). But the fault is not in the law; it is in the sinner who is a law-breaker, whereas the law – precisely because it is God's law and his standard of holiness, justness, goodness, and spirituality – is holy, just, good, and spiritual (*Romans* 7:12, 14), and it is glorious (*2 Corinthians* 3:7ff.). To keep God's law, then, is to be just before God.

Because they are law-breakers, sinners can never be justified by the law; they can only be condemned by it. A different principle of justification is needed if the sinner is to live before God. Yet the law is not set aside. On the contrary, it is perfectly fulfilled on the sinner's behalf by the incarnate Son, and his perfect fulfilling of the law was the essential preliminary to his atoning sacrifice on the cross; for it is solely on the basis of his faultless keeping of the law that the incarnate Son lives before God and that he qualified himself, as our fellow man, to suffer the death of the cross, the penalty of our law-breaking, as our substitute. Accordingly, Paul tells the Christians in Rome: "As by one man's disobedience many were made sinners, so by one man's obedience many will be made righteous" (*Romans* 5:19). And the very heart of the Gospel is that "God made him who knew no sin to be sin for our sake, so that in him we might become the righteousness of God" (*2 Corinthians* 5:21). Consequently, the Gospel principle for sinners is that they may live and be just before God only by faith-union with Christ, with whom alone as the sole law-keeper, God is well pleased (*Matthew* 3:17; 17:5; *Isaiah* 42:1; *John* 17:4; *Ephesians* 1:6f.; *2 Peter* 1:17). "We hold," Paul declares, "that a man is justified by faith apart from works of law" (*Romans* 3:28); and again, in the *Galatian Epistle*, Paul insists that "a man is not justified by works of the law but through faith in Jesus Christ" (*Galatians* 2:16). As the sole "doer of the law" – the incarnate Son alone is just before God, and in him alone is the sinner's justification (*1 Corinthians* 1:30).

I wish to maintain, finally, that the evangelical doctrine that "a man is not justified by works of the law but by faith in Jesus Christ" applies not only to works done prior to regeneration but also to works done after regeneration. My argument is based on the Biblical teaching that the good works of the Christian believer are still works of the law. The promise of the new covenant includes the assurance: "I will put my law within them, and I will write it upon their hearts" (*Jeremiah* 31:33); and: "I will put a new spirit within them; I will take the stony heart out of their flesh, and give them a heart of flesh, that they may walk in my statutes and keep my ordinances and obey them" (*Ezekiel* 11:19ff.). This promise is fulfilled in and through him who is the Mediator of the new covenant, Jesus Christ (*Hebrews* 8:6ff.; *2 Corinthians* 3:3). For the believer, then, the law is still operative; not, however, as the way to justification, but as the way to sanctification; not as an external ordinance condemning him as a law-breaker (for he is justified through faith in Jesus Christ) , but written within his heart, so that he now delights in God's law and by the grace of the Holy Spirit is enabled to perform it. His life becomes a life of "faith working through love" (*Galatians* 5:6); for love is the sun of the law, which requires us to love God and to love our neighbour (*Matthew* 22:36-40; *Galatians* 5:14; *James* 2:8), and love therefore is the fulfilling of the law (*Romans* 13:8-10). The law no longer operates from without by the compulsion of command but from within by the impulse of love; and this is how it should have been from the beginning, when man was created in the image of his maker to enjoy the harmony of will and fellowship with his sovereign Lord.

It follows that the good works of the believer are the same as the good works enjoined by the law. But they are the good works of his sanctification, not of his justification. To speak of a necessity of these good works for our salvation, to relate them to "standing justified before the Lord," is to transpose them from the sphere of sanctification to the sphere of justification; and this, in the degree to which it is done, is to assign to them that very justifying status as works of the law which Paul has repudiated. It is to revert to that position which those who have assented to the Report professed to reject. It is to make the believer's salvation dependent in a real sense on his good works: hence the postulation of the notion of continuing justification and the notion of eschatological justification. Justification becomes some sort of process, fused with sanctification, instead of a divine once-for-all *fiat*.

This is confusion! And confusion, though certainly not intended, since it affects the true heart of the Gospel of our Lord Jesus Christ, that can only be expected to lead to the gravest consequences. It does not suffice to qualify the works of the believer as non-meritorious. Our justification is by faith apart from works; for, I repeat, the *only* works that contribute to, or are in any way necessary for, a person's justification are the works of the incarnate Son, who alone has kept the law, who therefore alone lives before God, and the perfect righteousness of whose works is imputed to the believing sinner. Our justification is complete and final in Christ, and must be so as it is his perfect holiness that is imputed to us. It is the root from which the fruit of Christian sanctification springs as the holiness of Christ is increasingly manifested in our lives. But sanctification is progressive precisely because, even though the believer by the grace of God now wills to do the will of God, his life is not here free from sin and self; hence John's admonition to Christian believers, that "if we say we have no sin we deceive ourselves," but that if we confess our sins God is faithful and just to forgive us and the blood of Jesus will cleanse us from all sin (1 John 1:7-9). Let us not, then, speak of a necessity of any works other than those of Christ for our justification. And let us look forward joyfully to our glorification, when, meeting our Master face to face and seeing him as he is, we shall at last be fully conformed to the perfection of his likeness (1 John 3:2ff.). Then at last, and only then, at our glorification, will our sanctification be complete, because it will be forever commensurate with the perfection of our justification.

Having begun with faith, let us not end with works!

I have written this dissent with a sense of my own deficiencies of expression and understanding as I have sought to contribute to the discussion of this great and central truth of our justification as sinners before Almighty God, and for these deficiencies I ask forgiveness.

PHILIP E. HUGHES

Letter of Concern

May 4, 1981

Dear Friends of the Reformed Faith:

We are sending you a copy of the enclosed letter, with the purpose to carry on a witness to the doctrine of justification and related doctrines, as they are revealed in Scripture and expressed in the doctrinal standards of the Presbyterian and Reformed churches.

We are responding to views, which have been recently advanced, that emphasize the believer's good works as necessary for his justification. These and other problematic statements are being circulated and are causing confusion and division in the Reformed community. They raise critical doctrinal issues which must be resolved.

It is our hope that the churches will resist these divergent views and continue to hold clearly to the Reformed witness that the justification of sinners is by the imputation of Christ's righteousness, by grace alone, through faith alone.

Questions as to the relation of good works to justification have manifested themselves in various Reformed churches. For example, there have been problems in the examination of candidates for the ministry. In the Presbytery of Philadelphia of the Orthodox Presbyterian Church an intensive debate on the doctrinal issues, of more than two years, has brought no resolution but rather a practically even division of the Presbytery.

Within Westminster Theological Seminary there has been a long-standing controversy as to whether the sinner is justified by faith with its works or by faith apart from its works. The December 10-11, 1980 meeting of the Board of Trustees was faced with two reports from a commission appointed to recommend a resolution of the issue. One report recommended the exoneration of the professor whose views have been challenged but who has had the support of the majority of the Faculty. The other report recommended his dismissal. The Board divided in response to these reports: A motion for exoneration was defeated by a tie vote (11 to 11); then a motion to request the professor's resignation was defeated by a vote of 12 to 9; and finally the motion to exonerate, with the addition of reference to "all the advice and admonitions that the Board has previously made" to him "to be cautious and clear," was carried by a vote of 13 to 9.

Prior to this action the professor had not retracted his problematic statements. Indeed, when confronted with the fact that tapes of his class lectures in 1975 showed him teaching that, like faith, "good works are the instrument of justification," he admitted the statement was confusing although he defended his intention to be Reformed, but he did not retract the statement as erroneous.

We deplore this December 11th action. It is our conviction as trustees, Faculty members, alumni, and friends of Westminster Seminary and as members of the Reformed community, that this action makes it imperative for us to give a clear and unambiguous witness to the truth of the Gospel of grace, for the good of Westminster Seminary and of the Reformed and evangelical community.

The enclosed letter was signed by many of us and sent to each member of the Board of Trustees of Westminster Seminary in advance of the December 11th meeting. It presents a summary of issues which, we believe, continue to confront us all and which demand resolution.

Everett Bean	Robert D. Knudsen
Calvin K. Cummings	Arthur W. Kuschke
Donald C. Graham	David C. Lachman
W. Stanford Reid	R. Heber McIlwaine
Paul G. Settle	George W. Marston
George D. Sinclair	Albert N. Martin
Murray Forst Thompson	David J. Miller
Lester R. Bachman	Iain H. Murray
Henry W. Coray	Roger Nicole
Martin L. Dawson	Robert L. Reymond
Mariano DiGangi	O. Palmer Robertson
Clarence W. Duff	Douglas Rogers
David Freeman	H. Leverne Rosenberger
John P. Galbraith	C. Gregg Singer
W. Robert Godfrey	Leslie W. Sloat
Robert H. Graham	John C. Smith
William A. Haldeman	Morton H. Smith
Bruce F. Hunt	William J. Stanway
Mark W. Karlberg	Albert W. Steever, Jr.
Edward L. Kellogg	Douglas Vickers
Meredith G. Kline	Hugh P. Whitted, Jr.
Meredith M. Kline	William Young
George W. Knight, III	

P. S. The "Westminster Statement on Justification" has been widely circulated. That document appeared as the report of a committee of five, reporting to the Board in May, 1980. The minority report of that committee, signed by Messrs. Robertson and Settle, will be supplied on request.

Requests may be addressed to any of the following at P. O. Box 2070, Jenkintown, PA, 19046.

Calvin K. Cummings   Robert D. Knudsen
W. Stanford Reid   Arthur W. Kuschke

December 4, 1980

The Trustees of Westminster Theological Seminary

Dear Brethren:

For more than four years the controversy about the doctrinal position of the Rev. Norman Shepherd, Associate Professor of Systematic Theology, especially as to his teaching of the relation of the believer's works to justification, has continued without resolution. There has been no resolution of the problem either in the Seminary, or in the Presbytery of Philadelphia of the Orthodox Presbyterian Church. Statements endorsing Mr. Shepherd's position have been issued by a majority of the Faculty and by a majority of the Board of Trustees. The Seminary adopted in May of 1980 a statement on justification, which has been distributed as the *Westminster Statement on Justification*, but that statement does not deal with acknowledged problems in Mr. Shepherd's position and therefore does not meet the issue. On the other hand the Minority Report of May, 1980, signed by Messrs. Robertson and Settle, does meet the issue.

There are those on the Board and on the Faculty, as well as other representative Reformed scholars, who instead of being satisfied are deeply convinced that Mr. Shepherd's position is not only ambiguous but erroneous. Such men as William Hendriksen, Philip E. Hughes, D. Martyn Lloyd-Jones, Iain Murray, Roger Nicole, C. Gregg Singer, Morton Smith, and R. C. Sproul have read many of the papers by Mr. Shepherd and his critics and defenders, and have rejected his position.

In an attempt to settle the problem, the Board on December 10, 1980, will act on reports from a special commission, appointed by the Board in May of 1980, to recommend either Mr. Shepherd's exoneration or dismissal, as an end to the controversy.

We believe that the Board's decision on December 10 will be exceedingly critical. If Mr. Shepherd's position were to be endorsed at that meeting, a change would have come in Westminster's historic testimony.

The Seminary since its founding has become widely known for its unambiguous stand for the truth of the Scriptures, of the Reformed Faith, of the Gospel of grace. The endorsement of Mr. Shepherd's position would place upon the Seminary's testimony not only an ambiguity but a contradiction, as to the central doctrine of justification as well as to the doctrines of the covenant, of election, of reprobation, of grace, of faith, and of the assurance of the believer.

Although Mr. Shepherd has repeatedly affirmed his adherence to the Scriptures and to the Westminster standards, and has repeatedly assented to true formulations of the doctrines being debated, there remains a basic inconsistency because he has never repudiated many seriously misleading formulations which he has given to the Board and to the public. Even his defenders have considered them confusing. Nevertheless, in spite of some superficial corrections in his terminology his position has remained essentially the same. Many of his distinctive statements remain uncorrected. It is the continuing presence of a large mass of unrepudiated statements, which we consider to be erroneous in the light of the Reformed system of doctrine, which call forth our judgment that the basic doctrinal problems remain unresolved. And it is such distinctive statements by Mr. Shepherd which first produced, and have then continued the controversy.

We do not call into question Mr. Shepherd's motives or personal sincerity. We do question his theological consistency, and the position set forth by his distinctive and unrepudiated public doctrinal statements. The Seminary should not leave unresolved the great questions forced upon the Christian world by these statements.

We quote some of these statements which call forth our deep concern:

(Election and Reprobation Reversible, from Covenant Perspective)

"If the Exodus is the great election of Israel...the exile is the great rejection or reprobation of Israel.... Nevertheless precisely the rejected nation is once again elect. (*Isaiah* 14:1)"
- "Reprobation in Covenant Perspective, the Biblical Doctrine," page 13; a lecture at the Christian Reformed Ministerial Institute, Grand Rapids, June 1978.

"Now, what is true of the nation is also true of the person. Judas is introduced into the community, the covenant community of the elect, but he is rejected as a son of perdition because of his apostasy (*John* 17:12). We have the brother in *1 Cor.* 5, verses 1 through 5, addressed as one of the saints at Corinth but he is to be delivered to Satan because of his immorality. We have Simon of Samaria who believed (*Acts*

8:13), but becomes entangled in the bond of iniquity (verse 23).... Here we have elect persons who are excommunicated."
– "Reprobation in Covenant Perspective," page 9.

"There are, of course, hypocrites among the elect.... When the reprobate turn in repentance and faith, they are no longer looked upon as reprobate but as elect.... The Gospel calls upon the ungodly – the reprobate – to believe and be saved."
– *The Banner*, March 28, 1980, page 19.

"Reprobation from within the context of the covenant (please underline with about four lines that expression); reprobation from within the context of the covenant, that is to say, reprobation from the point of view of the covenant is not incontrovertible."
– "Reprobation in Covenant Perspective," page 12.

(*Our Knowledge of Election Is Through the Covenant*)

"God's election from the point of view of his decree – that stands firm. But that is [of] the secret things which belong to God. Our knowledge of election is through the covenant."
– "Reprobation in Covenant Perspective," page 10.

"All of Biblical language is covenant language...."
– "More on Covenant Evangelism," in *The Banner of Truth*, November, 1977, page 22.

"Paul speaks from the perspective of observable covenant reality and concludes from the visible faith and sanctity of the Ephesians that they are the elect of God."
– "The Covenant Context for Evangelism," in *The New Testament Student and Theology*, Volume III, 1976, page 63.

"*Ephesians* 1:1-14, *John* 15:1-8, and similar passages function as canon only within the context of the covenant."
— "The Covenant Context for Evangelism," page 65.

(*Extent of the Atonement*)

"The Reformed evangelist can and must say on the basis of *John* 3:16, Christ died to save you.... If the proclamation, Christ died to save you, be construed from the perspective of election it is at best only possibly true, and may well be false. From this perspective Christ did, indeed, die only for the elect and not for the reprobate. But *John* 3:16 is embedded in the covenant documents of the New Testament. As such it is not an elaboration of the doctrine of election as God views election or a commentary on the extent of the atonement in an absolute sense, but covenant truth. Its specific application – and this is what the proclamation of the Gospel must be – in the declaration, Christ died for you, is a manifestation of the grace of our Lord Jesus Christ opening the way to fellowship with God. As such, it calls men, each and every man, to that fellowship...."
— "The Covenant Context for Evangelism," page 62.

(*Baptism and Regeneration*)

"Third thesis: Baptism rather than regeneration is the point of transition from lostness in death to salvation in life."
— "The Covenant Context for Evangelism," page 66.

"I now sincerely regret the antithetical way in which I stated my third thesis.... The thesis would be better stated as follows: Baptism marks the point of transition from death to life.... We must also say, of course, that the passage from death to life occurs at conversion, or regeneration, or union with Christ. But as creatures we cannot know precisely the moment when this takes place. It may take place before, or after, or in conjunction with baptism; it may never take place at all. When, then, as far as the church is concerned, does a man become a Christian? Do we not have to say, when he is baptized?"

– "More on Covenant Evangelism," page 25.

"In contrast to regeneration-evangelism, a methodology oriented to the covenant structure of Scripture and to the Great Commission presents baptism as the point of transition from death to life... A sinner is not "really converted" until he is baptized.... Paul's Damascus road experience is usually thought of as the time of his conversion. The Bible does not say when he was regenerated, but it does say when he was baptized (*Acts* 9:18) and indicates that this was when his sins were washed away (*Acts* 22:16)."

– "The Covenant Context for Evangelism," page 71.

"In Scripture...the Christians are those who have been baptized; the unbelievers are those who have not been baptized."

– "The Covenant Context for Evangelism," page 72.

"The Great Commission is not given in either *Matthew* or *Luke* in terms of calling upon men to believe. Faith is not mentioned specifically, but only by implication. What is explicitly asserted is the call to repentance and good works.... All who have been baptized and are seeking to do the will of God are to be regarded as Christian brothers."

– "The Covenant Context for Evangelism," page 74.

(The Good Works of the Believer
Necessary to Justification)

"The exclusive ground of the justification of the believer in the state of justification is the righteousness of Jesus Christ, but his obedience, which is simply the perseverance of the saints in the way of truth and righteousness, is necessary to his continuing in a state of justification (*Heb.* 3:6, 14)."
> – "Thirty-four Theses on Justification in Relation to Faith, Repentance, and Good Works," November, 1978, Thesis 21.

"The righteousness of Jesus Christ ever remains the exclusive ground of the believer's justification, but the personal godliness of the believer is also necessary for his justification in the judgment of the last day (*Matt.* 7:21-23; 25:31-46; *Heb.* 12:14)."
> – "Thirty-four Theses," Thesis 22.

"… Good works, works done from true faith, according to the law of God, and for his glory, being the new obedience wrought by the Holy Spirit in the life of the believer united to Christ, though not the ground of his justification, are nevertheless necessary for salvation from eternal condemnation and therefore for justification *(Rom.* 6:16, 22; *Gal.* 6:7-9)."
> – "Thirty-four Theses," Thesis 23.

(After Repentance, the Doers of the Law
Will Be Justified)

"The Pauline affirmation in *Romans* 2:13, 'the doers of the law will be justified,' is not to be understood hypothetically in the sense that there are no persons who fall into this class, but in the sense that faithful disciples of the Lord Jesus Christ will be justified (Compare *Luke* 8:21; *James* 1:22-25)."

– "Thirty-four Theses," Thesis 20.

"The faith that justifies is the faith that works by love. But *Gal.* 5:6 is not an isolated phenomenon in Paul. The same thrust comes out elsewhere in various ways. An example of this is *Rom.* 2:13, 'for not the hearers of the law are just before God, but the doers of the law will be justified.' The knowledge that the doers of the law will be justified is not, by itself, of much comfort to guilty sinners. In fact, it is bad news…. In Rom. 2:13, Paul gives no comfort to those who do the works of the law. Rather, he calls all men, both Jew and Gentile to repentance…. There are those who do repent. When they repent they cease being evil-doers – here hearers of the law – and they become doers of the will of God…. By way of repentance men become doers of the law who will be justified and enter into eternal life (*Rom.* 2:7). 'Doers of the law' is a category to which no one belongs by nature for all have sinned and are under condemnation; but that sinners can become 'doers of the law' in the sense of Rom. 2:13 by grace is made abundantly evident in the Scriptures."

– "The Grace of Justification," February 8, 1979, pages 8-10.

* * * * * * * * * *

These quotations reflect a misreading of various aspects of the doctrine of the covenant. It is true that God the Creator graciously communicates with us, his creatures, by way of covenant. However, the distance between God and man does not mean that God is not the Author of truth, or that his grace as decreed for us is contradicted by his grace as covenantally revealed to us. He reveals, through his covenant, and to us in our covenant relationship, not only the very same gifts of saving grace which he himself eternally knows and gives, but he also reveals to us his promises that these gifts, once granted, will never fail. As creatures we do not know comprehensively, as God does. But all he reveals to us in his special revelation is revealed by way of covenant, and whatsoever he reveals is true.

It is not proper, therefore, to set up a dichotomy whereby according to God's secret will, election or justification cannot be lost, but according to our covenant perspective they may be lost. The statements cited show a tendency to use typically Calvinistic language with respect to the level of God's secret will, but in the level of "covenant perspective" to use typically Arminian language (Christ died for you; the elect may become reprobate). There is even the notion that *Ephesians* 1:1-14 does not "function as canon" in relation to God's unchangeable decree of predestination, but functions as canon only within that "context of the covenant" where "election" may be lost. This is a misreading of the doctrine of God's incomprehensibility. That doctrine does not mean that the perspicuously revealed grace of God in election and justification can be regarded as changeable on the covenant level.

Again, covenant obedience is enkindled by God's grace. We love him because he first loved us. Loving obedience is our response. And the covenant, here, is specifically the covenant of grace. By his grace we are brought into his covenant and freely justified, in order that we should then perform those good works which God has before ordained. But we should not turn our covenant obedience around to make it necessary in any way for our justification. This would be seeking our own righteousness, rather than the righteousness which is of God by faith. The justifying grace which puts us right with God is not of our works; lest any man should boast. "It is of faith, that it might be by grace" (*Romans* 4:16).

The statements that the believer's good works are necessary to justification, and that after repentance the doers of the law will be justified, appear to have much the same force as the Roman Catholic doctrine of justification: that is, of grace mingled with our obedience, or justification through sanctification, or justification by a faith which includes our works. We observe that, as we understand Reformed doctrine, covenant obedience, which is always obligatory upon those in the covenant of grace, and essential in our sanctification, is not required either for election or for justification. The only obedience which suffices for justification is that of Christ, imputed to us. If the believer must look to any degree to his own obedience for his justification, then his hope is lost.

Most of our attention, in the long debate, has been given to the doctrine of justification. Paul regarded this doctrine as so crucial as to reject any compromise of it in strong language– a fall from the doctrine of grace (*Gal.* 5:4), a frustrating of the grace of God, as though Christ were dead in vain (*Gal.* 2:21). Paul described the error he combated as seeking to be justified by the works of the law. Justification is by faith apart from the works of the law (*Rom.* 3:28). What are "the works of the law"? The works of the law are anything we do for our justification.

"It makes void the Gospel to introduce works in connection with justification" – John Murray, *Collected Writings*, Volume II, page 221. Calvin says, "But a great part of mankind imagine that righteousness is composed of faith and works" (*Institutes*, III:11:13). "Works do not enter the account of faith but must be utterly separated" (III:11:18). "Let us not consider works to be so commended after free justification that they afterward take over the function of justifying man, or share this office with faith" (III:17:9).

The issue has been stated clearly by Bavinck. "For the quarrel between Rome and the Reformation did not have to do with whether we are justified by an active or inactive faith, or by a living or a dead faith. But the question was, just as it was for Paul, whether faith with its works, or whether faith apart from its works, justifies us before God and in our consciences" (*Gereformeerde Dogmatiek*, volume IV, 4th edition, 1930, page 207). Either by faith with its works, or by faith apart from its works. Bavinck saw these as the alternatives. It seems to us that Mr. Shepherd endorses the former. Bavinck held to the latter.

We write for the record. On December 10th the Board should make a clear break with Mr. Shepherd's doctrinal position. The break should be unmistakable, so as to hold the Seminary to the historic testimony for which it was founded.

Henry W. Coray
Mariano DiGangi
Clarence W. Duff
David Freeman
Donald C. Graham
Edward L. Kellogg
Meredith G. Kline
Robert D. Knudsen

Arthur W. Kuschke
David C. Lachman
George W. Marston
W. Stanford Reid
Paul G. Settle
Leslie W. Sloat
William Young

Reason and Specifications Supporting the Action of the Board of Trustees in Removing Professor Shepherd

Approved by the Executive Committee of the Board, February 26, 1982

The Board of Trustees of Westminster Theological Seminary on November 20, 1981, acted pursuant to Article III, Section 15 of the Constitution of the Seminary to remove the Rev. Norman Shepherd as Associate Professor of Systematic Theology on the ground that the Board in its mature judgment had become convinced that such removal was necessary for the best interests of the Seminary. The action was taken upon the recommendation of a special Visitation Committee.

The Board also elected three Board members to serve with two members chosen by the Faculty on a Committee of Five charged to conduct a full investigation of the findings of the Visitation Committee and to give to Professor Shepherd abundant opportunity to defend his conduct of his office.

The Executive Committee, at the direction of the Board, prepared a brief statement of the reasons for the action. The statement said that: "The Board makes no judgment whether Mr. Shepherd's views as such contradict the Westminster Standards." But the statement also alleged that "partly because of deep inherent problems in the structure and the particular formulations of Mr. Shepherd's views, partly because of Mr.

Shepherd's manner of criticizing opponents as non-Reformed rather than primarily incorporating their concerns more thoroughly into his own position in response, too many people in the Seminary community and constituency and the larger Christian public have come to judge that Mr. Shepherd's teaching appears to them to contradict or contravene, either directly or impliedly, some element in that system of doctrine taught by the Standards."

The Committee of Five has judged that the allegations respecting "deep inherent problems in the structure and the particular formulations of Mr. Shepherd's views" and respecting his manner of responding to critics are not sufficiently specific to enable the Committee to do its work. It has, therefore, asked the Board to determine the procedure to be followed. It has further recommended that clear and explicit charges against Mr. Shepherd be drawn up together with specifications and that the Executive Committee draw up these charges and specifications.

Since the Board did not remove Mr. Shepherd on the ground of demonstrated errors in his teaching, charges of such errors, together with specifications, obviously would not be appropriate. The Executive Committee acknowledges, however, that Mr. Shepherd is entitled to a clear statement of the reason for his dismissal and presents this statement to him and to the Committee of Five as an attempt to clarify further the Board's action.

I. Statement of Reason for Removal

The Board has come to the decision that Prof. Shepherd's removal is necessary for the best interests of the Seminary with great regret, and only after seven years of earnest study and debate, because it has become convinced that Mr. Shepherd's teaching regarding justification, the covenant of works and the covenant of grace, and related themes is not clearly in accord with the teaching of Scripture as it is summarized in the system of doctrine contained in the Westminster Standards.

This reason is deemed by the Executive Committee to be "adequate cause" under the Tenure and Removal policy of the Board, and supports the finding that Mr. Shepherd's removal is necessary for the best interests of the Seminary under Article III, Section 15 of the Constitution. Although Mr. Shepherd was removed by the Board pursuant to Article III, Section 15 of the Constitution, the Board appointed the Committee of Five composed of both Faculty and Board members, in order to provide to Mr. Shepherd the procedural safeguards of the Tenure and Removal Policy. The Board has exercised its Constitutional authority to remove in light of these procedural safeguards in the Tenure and Removal Policy.

Westminster Theological Seminary exists primarily to prepare for the gospel ministry men "who shall truly believe, and cordially love, and therefore endeavor to propagate and defend in its genuineness, simplicity, and fullness, that system of religious belief and practice which is set forth in the *Westminster Confession of Faith* and *Catechisms...*" (*Catalogue*, 1981, p. 5; cf. *Charter*, Art. II). This creedal commitment rests on the conviction that these standards faithfully express the teaching of Scripture. Every Faculty member pledges not to "inculcate, teach or insinuate anything which shall appear to contradict or contravene, either directly or impliedly, any element in that system of doctrine..." (*Constitution*, Art. V. 3). The Policy Statement on Academic Freedom and Responsibility acknowledges that "Christian freedom exists within the confession of Christian faith" and notes that voting members of the Seminary faculty have voluntarily accepted the *Westminster Confession of Faith* and *Catechisms*. The authority of the Word of God binds the conscience even as it frees it from human tradition. Teachers are free, within their confessional commitment, to propose and discuss both tentative and settled convictions. A teacher must exercise this academic freedom, however, "with the recognition that there may be, in the public mind, a tacit representation of the Seminary in whatever he says or writes, whether as a teacher, as a scholar, or as an individual citizen. He should therefore at all times be accurate, and exercise appropriate restraint."

A professor of systematic theology at Westminster Seminary must be able to communicate with unmistakable clarity the doctrine of justification by sovereign grace alone through faith alone on the grounds of Christ's righteousness alone. Both the Board of the Seminary and its constituency must have full confidence that the Seminary's teaching is orthodox with respect to these truths which lie at the heart of the gospel.

After spending much time and effort in writing and speaking on these areas of theology, Mr. Shepherd has not been able to satisfy the Board and considerable portions of the Seminary constituency that the structure of his views and his distinctive formulations clearly present the affirmations by which our Standards guard the relation and place of faith and works with respect to salvation.

II. Specifications Regarding the History of the Controversy

The long controversy regarding the views and teaching of Mr. Shepherd began in the spring of 1975. The Presbytery of Ohio of the Orthodox Presbyterian Church delayed the licensure of Mr. David Cummings because of his unsatisfactory answers regarding the relation of good works to justification. Mr. Cummings believed that he was presenting the doctrine he had been taught in Mr. Shepherd's class in the fall of 1974. He alleges that Mr. Shepherd taught that "If justification presupposes repentance, it presupposes good works." "Justification is related to good works as justification is related to faith." At that time Mr. Shepherd in his class lectures outlined his reasoning as follows: Justification Presupposes Faith; Faith is not the Ground of Justification; Faith is the Instrument of Justification. Justification Presupposes Good Works; Good Works are not the Ground of Justification; Good Works are the Instrument of Justification.

In an informal meeting of the Faculty on April 14, 1975, Mr. Shepherd questioned making justification by faith alone a touchstone of orthodoxy, since, as he argued, what can be said of faith can also be said of good works; neither can be the ground of justification, both can be instrument.

The teaching of Mr. Shepherd at this time questioned or challenged the statements of the Westminster Standards: "Faith ... is the alone instrument of justification..." (*WCF* XI:2); "...only for the righteousness of Christ imputed to us, and received by faith alone" (*SC* Q. 33); "...not for any thing wrought in them, or done by them, but only for the perfect obedience and full satisfaction of Christ, by God imputed to them, and received by faith alone" (*LC* Q. 70); "...imputing his righteousness to them, and requiring nothing of them for their justification but faith, which also is his gift..." (*LC* Q. 71). (Compare *Heidelberg Catechism* Q. 60, 61; *Second Helvetic Confession* XVI:7: "Therefore, although we teach with the apostle that a man is justified by grace through faith in Christ and not through any good works, yet we do not think that good works are of little value and condemn them.")

When Mr. Shepherd was challenged by Faculty members and others concerning his views he presented a paper to the Faculty on October 1, 1976. A Faculty report to the February 10, 1977 meeting of the Board singled out expressions that were found troubling in the October paper, for example: "...faith coupled with obedience to Christ is what is called for in order to salvation and therefore in order to justification." "Thus, faith and new obedience are in order to justification and salvation." The Faculty report called attention to the responsibility of teachers to avoid confusing statements.

A fuller report of the Faculty was made to the Board meeting of May 17, 1977. The report acknowledged clarifications from Mr. Shepherd in an April 15, 1977 statement, but said that "Mr. Shepherd continues to defend views and expressions contained in the October 1976 study paper" and that earlier concerns had not been resolved. The Faculty concluded that "certain of Mr. Shepherd's statements on the subject of justification require further consideration and modification to avoid obscuring the teaching of Scripture and the Westminster Standards." Mr. Shepherd was no longer using the word "instrument" in reference to works but had suggested that "instrument" was not altogether a good term to describe faith either. Mr. Shepherd objected to making faith prior to justification in an "ordo salutis" as Charles Hodge (and John

Murray) had done. He suggested that if such an "ordo salutis" were to be constructed, good works should be inserted with faith and repentance before justification. (*Cf.* "The Relation of Good Works to Justification in the Westminster Standards," p. 22.) The Faculty report specified four areas where modifications of the language and formulations of Mr. Shepherd were to be desired. These concerned his broad use of the term justification, his language of requirement for good works in relation to justification (as against *LC* Q. 71), his reluctance to make faith prior to justification even in a logical sense; and his strategy of explaining the "alone" function of faith as separating it from meritorious works rather than from other graces.

Six members of the Faculty believed that these criticisms were not severe enough; they held Mr. Shepherd's views to be erroneous and sent their evaluation to the Board.

There followed many months of intensive study and discussion in a divided Faculty and Board. Mr. Shepherd was urged to "exercise great caution and restraint in his presentation of the doctrines of justification and good works in his teaching" (Board *Minutes*, May 24, 1977, p. 4). He was asked to modify certain statements and did so, but appealed for a better understanding of his statements in the light of his effort "to understand the application of redemption in terms of the dynamic of the covenant of grace" (*Response* to a Special Report of the Faculty...Jan. 3, 1978, p. 8). The Faculty, reading Mr. Shepherd's formulations in the light of his commendable concerns, concluded that his position did not contradict the system of doctrine taught in Scripture and summarized in the Standards. But the Faculty also concluded that the problem was not due solely to others' misunderstandings of his views. "Mr. Shepherd has exaggerated the basic position he is presenting by a method of polarization that attacks differing views so radically that his own views are caricatured. Further, his structure of argumentation seems bound to create misunderstanding. The faculty urges Mr. Shepherd for the cause of the kingdom, to seek less provocative language and different means of argument, less open to misunderstanding, to develop and explain his legitimate concerns." (April 25, 1978 Faculty report, p. 4).

The Board on May 23, 1978, defeated a motion to concur with the judgment of the report of the Faculty "that Mr. Shepherd's position, properly understood, does not undermine the unique role of faith in justification nor obscure the proper distinction between justification and sanctification, and is within the bounds of the Westminster Standards" (*Minutes*, p. 2). Instead, the Board, after hearing Mr. Shepherd, urged him to continue his study in the area and to report after a leave of absence granted to him.

At the November 14, 1978, Board meeting a motion that the formulation of Mr. Shepherd on the doctrine of justification be found not acceptable to the Board was defeated by one vote. This action followed another substantial Board interview with Mr. Shepherd, who had been invited to the last three Board meetings for discussions. He had been given a study leave for one year and was now urged to present to the Board before the February meeting a revised statement of his position.

On November 18, 1978, Mr. Shepherd presented "Thirty-four Theses on Justification in Relation to Faith, Repentance and Good Works" to the Presbytery of Philadelphia of the Orthodox Presbyterian Church. In a covering letter he said that a resolution of the problem no longer seemed possible in the limited context of the Seminary and that he was appealing to the church. These theses and his paper presented to the February, 1979 Board meeting ("The Grace of Justification") became the statements of his views by which he wished to be judged.

The Presbytery gave exhaustive consideration to the theses over many months, devoting ten full-day meetings to discussion and debate. Three of the theses were set aside as involving historical rather than theological judgments. The Presbytery as a Committee of the Whole found the other theses to be in harmony with the teaching of Scripture and the Reformed Standards, sometimes by a close vote. (In one case the vote of the Moderator broke a tie.) One thesis was declared to be permissible although the motion to find it in harmony failed. When the findings of the Committee of the Whole were reported to the Presbytery, a motion to adopt the report failed on a tie vote.

On February 8, 1979, the Board received Mr. Shepherd's paper "The Grace of Justification" and discussed it, along with the "Thirty-four Theses" presented to the Presbytery. After long discussion, the Board determined by a vote of 11-8 that it found no sufficient cause to pursue further its inquiries into Mr. Shepherd's teaching regarding justification by faith. His views, as presented to the Board, did not "call into question his adherence to the *Westminster Confession of Faith.*"

At the same time the Board urged Mr. Shepherd "to continue to give attention not only to precision in expressing Biblical doctrine but also to wisdom in communicating it. No doubt the substantial misunderstanding that has arisen offers sufficient warning to Mr. Shepherd of the importance of this counsel" (*Minutes*, pp. 3, 17).

The Board also urged Faculty discussion and interchange on the issues.

Continuing division produced more communications from Board and Faculty to the May 29, 1979 meeting of the Board. Ten Board members signed a statement that the Board had acted prematurely in February. A Committee of Five was erected, representing the two sides from Board and Faculty. The Committee was charged with preparing a study paper and statement on the doctrine of justification by faith. The Committee was directed to seek the counsel of Board, Faculty, and other theological scholars in discharging its task.

The Committee prepared the "Westminster Statement on Justification" which was approved by the Faculty on May 14, 1980, with some recommendations for improvement. The Board also in its meeting of May 27, 1980, approved the Statement with the recommendation included. Mr. Shepherd voted in the Faculty to approve the statement and has indicated his agreement with it, most recently in his October 8, 1981 letter to the Board: "I voted for its adoption and continue to affirm my full agreement with this statement."

In spite of this agreement the controversy was not resolved. Questions remain because of points at which the affirmations and denials of the statement seemed to run counter to Mr. Shepherd's writings. For example:

(1.) One of the primary points emphasized in the Sandy Cove lectures (July, 1981) is that the obedience required of Adam in the "Creation Covenant," had he rendered it, would not have been meritorious. Adam was a son, not a laborer. The concept of wages earned, reward merited, is not appropriate to the father-son relationship. This is not a point made somewhat incidentally by Mr. Shepherd along the way, but a point that is evidently fundamental in his theology of the covenant. And yet the "Westminster Statement on Justification" states: "That covenant has been called the covenant of works.... Although God's gracious goodness can be seen in the disproportion between the limited requirement and the eternal reward, the covenant required the obedience of faith as its condition. By that obedience the promised reward could be claimed as *merited*" (p. 9, underline added); and Mr. Shepherd says that he is in full agreement.

The Statement goes on to say: "Only Christ, the second Adam, could atone for sin by the sacrifice of himself and *merit* the covenant reward." Mr. Shepherd's understanding of the nature of covenant relationship, father-son relationship, insists that the idea of meriting a reward is not appropriate to such a relationship, and yet he has affirmed full agreement with the Westminster Statement.

(2.) The Westminster Statement affirms "the necessary *causal priority* of God's justification of the sinner to the existence in him of any new obedience that is acceptable to God" (p. 15). In Thesis 23 of the "Thirty-four Theses on Justification," Mr. Shepherd has argued that "good works... being the new obedience wrought by the Holy Spirit in the life of the believer united to Christ" are "necessary... for justification." This Thesis seems to many readers to affirm the causal priority of new obedience to justification, which is to reverse the order affirmed in the Seminary statement.

(3.) The Westminster Statement denies "that justifying faith can be defined properly so that it virtually includes in its essence the new obedience which faith inevitably produces" (p. 15). Thus it goes on to "affirm that in that aspect of the gospel's call which is specifically for justification the sinner must be

141

called to believe in Christ; this call may be expressed in a summons to follow Christ, but only when that following is presented as the evidence and fruit of faith; and we deny that the summons to believe specifically for justification and the summons to follow Christ in faith, repentance and new obedience are ultimately the same thing" (p. 17). The thrust of this affirmation and this denial appears to be clearly at odds with the thrust of Prof. Shepherd's argument in "The Covenant Context of Evangelism": "It is both striking and significant that the Great Commission is not given in either *Matthew* or *Luke* in terms of calling upon men to believe. Faith is not mentioned specifically, but only by implication. What is explicitly asserted is the call to repentance and good works. When the call to faith is isolated from the call to obedience, as it frequently is, the effect is to make good works the supplement to salvation or simply the evidence of salvation" (*The New Testament Student and Theology*, Presbyterian and Reformed: 1976, p. 74).

In the course of the work of the committee drafting the Statement, two members solicited the opinion of various scholars regarding Mr. Shepherd's written views. Some evaluations were positive on the whole, but most expressed concern or alarm. These included William Hendriksen, Roger Nicole, Morton Smith, Iain H. Murray, Gregg Singer, R. C. Sproul, and Martyn Lloyd-Jones as well as scholars having some relation to the Seminary including Meredith Kline, Philip E. Hughes, and W. Stanford Reid.

The Board in its May 27, 1980 meeting determined

> that in view of:
> a. continuing allegations by members of the faculty and board that Professor Shepherd's teaching is misleading and tends to confuse the doctrines of justification by

faith alone and other doctrines central to the doctrinal basis of the seminary; and

b. documentation presented to this board meeting purporting to support such charges; and

c. the broader scope of doctrinal issues raised, including the question of our understanding of the covenants and the covenantal perspective in Biblical teaching; and

d. the seriousness with which Professor Shepherd's alleged misrepresentations and confusing structures of thought are viewed by those who are concerned;

the board erect a commission to determine whether the charges made against Professor Shepherd's views are substantial and true, and to determine whether his published views and classroom lectures do confuse in a serious fashion the system of doctrine to which the seminary is committed, and to discover his present opinion on the issues that have been controverted, all with a view to determining a recommendation to be made to the board by the commission at a special meeting of the board in November, 1980; such a recommendation should either propose that Mr. Shepherd be dismissed or that he be exonerated and the controversy ended in the faculty and board;

and that the commission be composed of three board members chosen by the board and three faculty members chosen by the faculty, together with the chairman of the board as a voting member;

and that Mr. Shepherd be required to meet with the commission at its request on dates mutually satisfactory, and that Mr. Shepherd be entitled to counsel of his choosing when hearings are held by the commission;

and that the commission be authorized to seek such other information or testimony as it shall judge to be necessary for its task.

A special meeting of the Board was held December 10-11, 1980, to receive and act upon the report of this Commission. Four members of the Commission reported that the Commission had formulated allegations to present to Mr. Shepherd, had heard him, with his counsel, present his answers to the allegations for about nine hours in two days, and recommended that Mr. Shepherd be exonerated. Three other members of the Commission presented a lengthy report supporting the actions of dismissal or request for resignation. The issue was discussed at length by the Board with Mr. Shepherd and his counsel present. A motion to exonerate was lost on a tie vote, 11-11. The following motion was then passed:

> That on the bases of discussions with Mr. Shepherd and on the bases of other corroborating evidence, the board determines that Mr. Shepherd be exonerated from the allegation of holding views which are not in conformity with Scripture and the doctrinal standards of the seminary. All the advice and admonitions that the board has previously made to Mr. Shepherd to be cautious and clear are herewith restated.

The Board also recommended that a theological colloquium be organized by the Deans of the campuses.

Before the May 26, 1981 meeting of the Board the issue of Mr. Shepherd's views was again brought to the fore by the mailing of a letter to a wide list of church sessions and individuals. The letter was signed by 45 theologians and ministers and included a copy of another letter addressed to the Board before its meeting of December 10, 1980. The President deplored the mailing of this letter to the general public rather than to the Board and Faculty. He reported that concern about the soundness of the Seminary was spreading among the constituents of the Seminary, producing a critical situation.

The Board, on recommendation of the President, erected a committee of three trustees as a Visitation Committee to interview as necessary members of the Seminary community and to prepare recommendations "with a view to resolving the differences that have arisen among us and to restoring the good name of the Seminary." It was suggested that the Committee might organize a colloquium that might give some of the theologians who signed the letter the opportunity to discuss these issues with members of the Faculty.

The Visitation Committee reported to the November 20-21, 1981 meeting of the Board that it had solicited opinions and suggestions from board members, faculty, and staff of all three campuses, had conducted phone interviews, and had met with 17 faculty and staff members, gathering information and seeking reconciliation. Meetings were held with representative students as well. An attempt was made to hold a colloquium that would include Professor Gaffin, J. I. Packer, R.C. Sproul, R. Nicole, Morton Smith, Carl W. Bogue and others. Professor Shepherd first agreed to participate, then refused on the ground that the inclusion of those who had opposed his views would have the effect of putting him on trial. Since reconciliation with some who had criticized his views was necessary to reverse the divisions that had been created and to restore the good name of the Seminary, the Committee would not agree to a colloquium without the participation of some of these critics. (No critics were proposed whose viewpoint was regarded as so fixed in opposition as to impede reasonable discussion or conciliation.)

In spite of Mr. Shepherd's refusal to participate in the colloquium, the Visitation Committee was encouraged by its meeting with him on August 21, 1981. It appeared to members of the Committee that Mr. Shepherd was willing to withdraw statements that had created confusion and to make corrections and amends as recommended in some of the letters that had been received.

The statement presented by Mr. Shepherd to the Committee on October 9 was a disappointment to the Committee. Mr. Shepherd stated that his views had been misinterpreted, misrepresented, and misunderstood. While he did not claim to work without fault, he apologized only "to the extent that my statements have caused misunderstanding."

The Committee also requested an evaluation from President Clowney as to the current status of the theological problem. Mr. Clowney reported on controversial elements in Mr. Shepherd's views.

The Committee summarized its findings regarding division over Mr. Shepherd's views in the Faculty and Board, among outside theologians, pastors and constituents. It noted certain ecclesiastical repercussions. The Committee then recommended the removal of Professor Shepherd.

The Faculty communicated to the Board a series of motions with respect to the report of the Visitation Committee. With Mr. Shepherd participating, it voted 7-4 with 3 abstentions to ask the Board not to remove Mr. Shepherd. A motion to "affirm that Mr. Shepherd's distinctive emphases and teaching are in accordance with the system of doctrine taught in Scripture and subscribed to in the subordinate standards of the Seminary" was amended to "affirm that Mr. Shepherd's system of theology is not out of accord with the system of doctrine taught in Scripture and subscribed to in the subordinate standards of the Seminary." This amended motion was carried with one negative vote.

At a meeting of the Board on November 20-21, 1981, the recommendation of the Visitation Committee that Mr. Shepherd be removed from his office for the good of the Seminary as provided for in the Constitution was discussed at length with Mr. Shepherd present. He was again heard by the Board. A letter in which he defended himself was also presented to the Board. The Board then acted to remove Mr. Shepherd, to erect a committee to investigate the findings of the Visitation Committee "giving Professor Shepherd abundant opportunity to defend his conduct of his office" and to suspend Mr. Shepherd until the investigation should be completed and his removal became effective. The action was passed by a majority of the entire membership of the Board. (13 yes, 8 no, 1 abstention).

The Board then directed the Executive Committee to prepare a statement giving the terms of reference for the Committee of Five. (This statement is appended.) Mr. Shepherd's present remuneration was continued through June, 1983, or until he has had other full-time employment for six months, whichever is sooner.

The long history of the controversy reveals how deeply disturbed members of the Faculty, Board, and constituency became with respect to Mr. Shepherd's views. It also shows the abundant opportunities that were afforded Mr. Shepherd to clarify his views and to remove misunderstandings. Mr. Shepherd was able to reassure a majority of the Faculty, and of the Board that his views were not in error, but the repeated admonitions for caution and clarity show that his expressions fell short of assuring these groups that his teaching was in full accord with the doctrinal standards of the Seminary.

Mr. Shepherd has modified and refined some statements of his views. He no longer teaches that works are co-instrumental with faith for justification (Letter to the Board, October 8, 1981; class lectures, "The Doctrine of the Holy Spirit," Tape 34). He conceded that there may be some form of logical priority for faith in relation to justification ("Response..." Jan. 3, 1978, p. 8). He has reworded the sentences in the October 1977 paper to which exception was taken and wishes to distance himself from that paper ("A Further Response..." March 1, 1978). Nevertheless, he has continued to defend his earlier statements in their context, as he did for example in the hearing before the commission that reported to the December 10-11, 1980 meeting of the Board ("Report to the Board ... from Three Members of the Commission," Nov. 19, 1980, p. 2). Further, he has continued to assert and develop his distinctive views in various lectures and articles, for example in "The Covenant Context for Evangelism," Beaver Falls, 1975; "Reprobation in Covenant Perspective," Grand Rapids, June, 1978; "The Biblical Doctrine of Reprobation," *The Banner*, March 21, 1980; "Life in Covenant with God," Sandy Cove, Md., July, 1981.

III. Problematics in Mr. Shepherd's Views

In spite of modifications that Mr. Shepherd has made in his expressions, the Board finds that the problems in his teaching are not resolved, and that they are inherent in his view of the "covenant dynamic." Although Mr. Shepherd appeals to the history of Reformed covenantal theology to support his position, the Board finds that Mr. Shepherd's construction is distinctive. It is in the distinctive elements and emphases of his theology of the covenant that the problem appears.

1. In his "covenant dynamic" Mr. Shepherd develops a formula that permits him to join good works to faith as the characteristic and qualifying response to grace. Obedience is the proper, full, and comprehensive term for all covenantal response, and specifically for our response in the covenant of grace. "A single word that commends itself from the history of redemption as a summary of covenantal response is the word 'obedience.'" "Covenant obedience passes over into the New Testament as the qualifying response to the gospel of grace" ("Doctrine of the Holy Spirit," Tape 31: "Faith as Covenant Response"). "We must be faithful to our promise to God. That's our faithfulness, or simply our faith." Mr. Shepherd urges that Paul in citing *Habakkuk* 2:4, is declaring that "the righteous shall live by his faithfulness," that is, in the covenantal loyalty and obedience that has faith as its leading and qualifying feature or element (*ibid.*).

Faith in the narrow sense is then a focus in the unified covenantal response of faithfulness; faith is itself a work ("Doctrine of Holy Spirit," Tape 22), an act of obedience within the total response of obedience. As obedience characterizes and qualifies the covenant response of Christ, so does it qualify our covenant obedience, for he is our pattern and example. He is the covenant Head, and "we are involved with him in the same covenant." "As the Sin-Bearer, bearing the sins of the world, he cast himself upon the mercy of the faithful Judge. That is exactly what we are enabled to do in him" ("Doctrine of Holy Spirit," Tape 31). "The covenant keeper *par excellence* is Jesus Christ, himself, the seed of Abraham, obedient unto death, even the death of the cross (*Philippians* 2:8). It is just in the way of covenant-keeping, after the pattern of Jesus Christ that the promises of the covenant are to be realized" ("The

Covenant Context for Evangelism," *The N.T. Student and Theology*, 1976, pp. 55f.).

The works to be distinguished from faith in the Pauline passages are not good works, but works of the flesh, works that are done to provide a meritorious ground of justification ("Doctrine of Holy Spirit," Tape 37: "Paul's Positive Estimate of Good Works," *cf.* Tape 20). Faith must not be abstracted from good works. Since faith, repentance, and good works are intertwined as covenantal response, and since good works are necessary to justification, the "ordo salutis" would better be: regeneration, faith/repentance/new obedience, justification ("The Relation of Good Works to Justification," p. 22). But it is better still, as Mr. Shepherd sees it, to set aside the puzzle of an individual *ordo salutis* and affirm the corporate and covenantal concept of our total response to grace ("Doctrine of the Holy Spirit," Tape 3: "Covenant and the Application of Redemption – Concept of the *Ordo Salutis*, Oriented to the Model of Adult Conversion," *cf.* Tape 4.).

Mr. Shepherd clearly affirms that neither our works nor our faith can ever be the ground of our justification. Indeed, he argues that faith cannot be the ground precisely because it is a work, something that we do ("Doctrine of Holy Spirit," Tape 22). But his development of the "covenantal dynamic" so unites faith with good works that while he is willing to affirm that good works are the *fruit* of faith, he prefers the language of accompaniment or of a "working faith." Both faith and good works are alike fruits of the Spirit, and are not to be thought of in sequence ("Doctrine of Holy Spirit," Tapes 24, 34).

The difficulty is that while he acknowledges that faith has a function distinct from that of the other graces (love, for example), this distinction is not important for the covenantal dynamic that he emphasizes. In lecturing on faith he treats first the " covenantal perspective" in which faith must be seen ("Doctrine of Holy Spirit," Tape 31). In that "covenantal perspective" obedience receives the covenantal blessing and faith functions as a focus of that obedience. The confessional emphasis on faith as the alone instrument of justification is muted in the "covenant dynamic" accent. The Westminster Standards emphasize faith alone, not merely in contrast to self-righteous works but in contrast to all that we might do. Justification rests on Christ's righteousness alone and faith looks away from one's self to Christ.

2. The "covenant dynamic" of Mr. Shepherd makes the function of our obedience in the covenant to be the same as the function of the obedience of Adam in the covenant before the fall ("Life in Covenant with God," Tapes 1, 2). Mr. Shepherd finds one covenantal pattern in all of Scripture. The pattern joins God's free grace and our response in faithful obedience. God addresses to us the promise of the covenant; accompanying the promise there is always a command. This relationship is as fundamental as divine sovereignty and human responsibility. The "dynamic" of that relationship, namely that God's sovereignty does not contradict but establishes our responsibility, is the fundamental dynamic of the covenant in Mr. Shepherd's view. In this "dynamic" God's grace is sovereign but not irrespective of our obedience; on the other hand grace is not conditioned on obedience "in an absolute sense." "What we have by grace is ours in the way of covenant loyalty and fidelity. That is to say, God does not by-pass the covenant in the application of redemption" ("Doctrine of Holy Spirit," Tape 34). He therefore stresses that every covenant has two sides, in this case, God's covenant faithfulness to us and our covenant

faithfulness to God. Because God's faithfulness comes first and provides for ours, no faithfulness or obedience on our part can be meritorious. Adam's covenantal obedience in the garden did not merit any reward; neither does our covenantal obedience ("Life in Covenant with God," Tape 1). But both are required by the covenant command. The threat for disobedience is eternal death. This threat is as real for us as it was for Adam in the garden ("Life in Covenant with God", Tape 2). The warnings of the New Testament (such as those cited by Mr. Shepherd in his letter to the Board of October 8, 1981) must not be blunted or made hypothetical in any way. God's threat to Adam or to Israel was not idle, and the same sanction of the covenant is directed against us in the New Covenant.

The difficulty here does not lie with Mr. Shepherd's assumptions regarding Divine sovereignty and human responsibility, common to the Reformed tradition and emphasized at Westminster Seminary. Neither does it lie with the use of covenantal language to describe the fundamental religious relation between the Creator-Father and Adam, the son of God, made in his image. The difficulty lies in failing to do justice to the history of redemption, to the distinctiveness of God's administration with Adam and to the distinctiveness of the New Covenant in Jesus Christ.

God's command to Adam and Eve regarding the tree of the knowledge of good and evil and their later expulsion from the tree of life in the garden have been understood in Reformed theology as constituting a period of probation for Adam as the first Head of the human race. If Adam had obeyed he would have been justified, confirmed in righteousness, and made heir to eternal life. Parallel to the doctrine of the imputation of Adam's sin runs the assumption of the imputation of Adam's righteousness to his descendants had he obediently fulfilled his probation (*WCF* VII:2). The term "merit" may be used in many senses. To affirm merit in the sense of a divinely recognized and imputable righteousness is not to deny man's dependence upon God nor to make man an autonomous bargainer with God. Had Adam obeyed, he would have been justified on the ground of his own inherent righteousness, not on the ground of the righteousness of another, as Mr. Shepherd recognizes.

Theological constructions respecting the probation of Adam may have uncertainties, but the analogy by which they are developed is the clear doctrine of the New Testament regarding Jesus Christ, the Second Adam. As the Westminster Standards teach, the covenant of grace is made with Christ and with the elect in him. He is the only Mediator of the New Covenant. He has borne the judgment, the wrath due to us, not simply as sinners, but as covenant-breakers.

Further, Christ's active obedience has fulfilled all righteousness for us. In Christ we have sustained our probationary period: It was for us that he was tempted in the wilderness, took the cup in the garden of Gethsemane, remained on the cross, suffered and died.

To describe our covenantal situation in analogy to Adam in the garden is dangerously misleading unless the radical difference that has taken place through the work of Christ our covenant-keeper is made clear. Yet in his Sandy Cove lectures on "Life in Covenant with God" Mr. Shepherd does the former without doing the latter. He describes the requirement of our covenant-keeping obedience in terms drawn from his description of Adam's covenant-keeping. We have resources that Adam did not have, Mr. Shepherd shows. We have forgiveness of sins in the blood of Christ; we have the Spirit to move us to obey; but we also have the same covenant condition to meet, and the same threat for disobedience. On the other hand, in these five lectures on the covenant Mr. Shepherd does not present the significance of Christ's keeping of the covenant for us.

Indeed, he mentions Christ's keeping of the law for us only incidentally in a context where he raises a question:

"Sometimes we say that there are really two ways of salvation. On the one hand, if you keep the law absolutely perfectly without making any mistakes, then you will be saved. But most of us recognize that we can't do that and so we look to Jesus Christ to keep the law for us. Now, I appreciate the gospel thrust of that, and it is right in a certain way, but think again my brothers and sisters. Let the Israelite observe the Mosaic law perfectly, to the letter, without making a single mistake. Will he be saved? No. Because the law is powerless to save" (Tape 3).

The omission of any clear treatment of Christ as the covenant Head, of his active obedience, of the imputation of his righteousness in the fulfillment of the covenant command, of his probation in our place (this in a treatment of the covenant that professes to be distinctively Reformed, after years of discussion) evidences a lack of clarity that cannot but cause concern.

Mr. Shepherd has met such criticism in a way that adds to the confusion. He assumes that those who criticize his view are falling away into antinomianism; that to emphasize that Christ has fulfilled the covenant for us is to take us "off the hook." Yet this is precisely the issue that the Westminster Standards so carefully define. They do it by showing how the law, revealing God's will and righteousness, remains the norm for our obedience even though believers are delivered from it as a covenant of works "so as thereby they are neither justified nor condemned" (LC Q. 97).

The WCF teaches that the threatenings of the law are of use to the regenerate "to show what even their sins deserve, and what afflictions in this life they may expect for them, although freed from the curse thereof threatened in the law" (WCF XIX:6). Mr. Shepherd insists that the threat of the curse is a necessary part of the covenant structure for Adam, for Israel, and for us. It promises blessing for the faithful and curse for the unfaithful. He has described the reservation that the threat of eternal death does not apply to believers as a "moral influence" theory of the warnings of Scripture (Faculty conference, October 26, 1981). He urged before the Board that just as Adam's posterity would not be "off the hook" if Adam had obeyed, but would be bound to fulfill the condition of obedience, so the posterity of Christ are not "off the hook."

The Larger Catechism states that the special use of the moral law for the regenerate that believe in Christ is "to show them how much they are bound to Christ for his fulfilling it, and enduring the curse thereof in their stead, and for their good; and thereby to provoke them to more thankfulness and to express the same in their greater care to conform themselves thereunto as the rule of their obedience" (LC Q. 97).

According to the Westminster Standards, the Bible teaches that Christ has fulfilled the covenant command for us and that we are therefore "off the hook" of the covenant of works (WCF XIX:6; LC Q. 97). Our obedience to Christ springs from gratitude for his salvation.

Mr. Shepherd rejects not only the term "covenant of works" but the possibility of any merit or reward attaching to the obedience of Adam in the creation covenant. He holds that faithful obedience is the condition of all covenants in contrast to the distinction made in the *Westminster Confession.* The *Westminster Confession* states in Chapter XII that the first covenant "was a covenant of works wherein life was promised to Adam, and in him to his posterity, upon condition of perfect and personal obedience." In contrast, in the second covenant, the covenant of grace, the Lord "freely offereth unto sinners life and salvation by Jesus Christ, requiring of them faith in him, that they may be saved." The covenant of works was conditioned upon perfect, personal obedience. The covenant of grace provides the obedience of Jesus Christ and therefore does not have our obedience as its *condition* but requires only faith in Christ to meet the demand of God's righteousness.

By rejecting the distinction between the covenant of works and the covenant of grace as defined in the Westminster Standards, and by failing to take account in the structure of the "covenantal dynamic" of Christ's fulfillment of the covenant by his active obedience as well as by his satisfaction of its curse, Mr. Shepherd develops a uniform concept of covenantal faithfulness for Adam, for Israel, and for the New Covenant people. The danger is that both the distinctiveness of the covenant of grace and of the new covenant fullness of the covenant of grace will be lost from view and that obedience as the way of salvation will swallow up the distinct and primary function of faith. Obedience is nurtured by faith in Christ and flourishes precisely as we trust wholly in him.

3. Mr. Shepherd's covenantal dynamic recasts the Confessional doctrine of assurance.

Mr. Shepherd applies the "covenantal dynamic" to the issues of election and assurance of salvation. He stresses that the covenant offers promise, not presumption. We do not have *information* about election. We cannot see our names in the Lamb's book of life. That would be information outside the sphere of faith ("Doctrine of the Holy Spirit," Tape 22). Assurance is assurance of the faithfulness of God's promise. "Faithlessness always sacrifices the promises" ("Doctrine of Holy Spirit," Tape 22).

We can know our election only in the perspective of the covenant, that is, as promise, but promise that will be sacrificed if we are faithless. Mr. Shepherd affirms that God's decretive election cannot fail, but since we cannot know God's decrees, the election that we know may be lost and may become reprobation through covenant-breaking. "God's election from the point of view of his decree – that stands firm. But that is (of) the secret things which belong to God. Our knowledge of election is through the covenant" ("Reprobation in Covenant Perspective," p. 10).

Election and reprobation from within the context of the covenant are not incontrovertible. We need to learn "covenant consciousness" of election from Israel. Israel knew that God is faithful to the faithful, to those who keep covenant, and that election is the foundation for covenant command and warning. Israel knew that God destroyed a generation in the wilderness for faithlessness to his covenant ("Life in Covenant with God," Tape 2). From this same covenantal perspective, according to Mr. Shepherd, justification can be lost. If one does not persevere in covenantal obedience, he will not continue in a state of justification (Theses 21, 23). Those whom God elects and justifies cannot lose their election or fall from a state of justification ("Doctrine of Holy Spirit," Tape 24). But we do not have information about God's decrees. We know our election only in the context of covenant. Our situation differs from Israel's not in that the threat of losing the promised inheritance is not real, but in that we can walk in the Spirit while Israel could walk only in the flesh ("Doctrine of Holy Spirit," Tape 30).

Mr. Shepherd conceives of his view as strengthening assurance. He contrasts it with speculating about one's election or becoming disturbed by self-examination in an effort to gain assurance through observing the fruits of election and regeneration. Instead he would point to "observable covenant reality." The elect are those who have been baptized, the members of the covenant community who are walking in the way. Some of the elect in this covenantal sense become reprobate, like Judas. Unbelievers are reprobate, but "when the reprobate turn in repentance and faith, they are no longer looked upon as reprobate but as elect..." (*The Banner*, March 28, 1980, p. 19).

Mr. Shepherd emphasizes that God's promise cannot fail but that passages like *John* 10:28 cannot be heard as information but as promise. Further, to reason that the warnings of the New Testament about perishing are hypothetical for the elect, is to make the exhortations to perseverance meaningless. This is "logicism and deductivism and a failure to appreciate the dynamic, the genius of the covenant" ("Holy Spirit" lectures, tape 38). Mr. Shepherd warns that we never move to a storm-free area. The promises of assurance do not mean that we are out of danger, that we cannot fall. They mean that Jesus will never lose a single one for whom he died. These are the elect known to God. We embrace that assurance, not as information, but as promise in faith.

Mr. Shepherd's interpretation of the covenant dynamic contrasts with the use of the covenant in this connection in the Westminster Standards. In the Westminster Standards God's decree and covenant are joined as expressing the immutability and certainty of God's giving the grace of perseverance to his elect: "This perseverance of the saints depends not upon their own free will, but upon the immutability of the decree of election, flowing from the free and unchangeable love of God the Father; upon the efficacy of the merit and intercession of Jesus Christ; the abiding of the Spirit, and of the seed of God within them; and the nature of the covenant of grace: from all which ariseth also the certainty and infallibility thereof" (*WCF* XVII:2). Mr. Shepherd, seeking to avoid "deductivism," declares that *WCF* XVII:2 does not describe a state of affairs but is a confession of faith. The "we" language of confession is not used, he recognizes, but is present by implication. He points to the term covenant of grace in *WCF* XVII:2 and assumes that it makes reference to our response. But it is the sovereignty of God's covenantal mercy that the *Confession* has in view. God makes an everlasting covenant with true believers. The *Larger Catechism* makes this sense clear: "True believers by reason of the unchangeable love of God, and his decree and covenant to give them perseverance, their inseparable union with Christ, his continual intercession for them, and the Spirit and the seed of God abiding in them, can neither totally nor finally fall away from the state of grace, but are kept by the power of God through faith unto salvation" (*LC* Q. 79).

Mr. Shepherd properly emphasizes the need of perseverance. God's decree of election assures that perseverance. The difficulty lies in the way in which the "covenantal dynamic" undercuts the infallible assurance of which the *Confession* speaks. Mr. Shepherd rightly declares that assurance is based on the word of God's promise, but in his desire to give full force to the threats of Scripture as applicable to believers, he fails to take account of the "informational" aspect of assurance through the witness of the Holy Spirit, in and with the Word, that we are children of God (*Rom.* 8:16; *WCF* XVIII; *LC* Q. 80). The Westminster Standards describe the infallible assurance that may be gained "without extraordinary revelation" (*WCF* XVIII:3; *LC* Q. 80). This clearly indicates on the one hand, that special revelation apart from the Word is not given to be the ground of assurance, but that on the other hand the knowledge and assurance that is gained is of the kind that could be produced by special revelation. Faith in God's promise is essential, of course, but faith and knowledge are not opposed in Scripture.

When the promise of God is put in the covenantal context as Mr. Shepherd presents it, the promise is accompanied by the threat, and the "dynamic" insists that the threat cannot be removed by a sure knowledge of salvation.

Mr. Shepherd has developed his distinctive system of "covenant dynamic" to achieve many commendable purposes. He desires to give full weight to the warnings of Scripture, to overcome an "easy-believism" in gospel preaching that would suppress the claims of the Lordship of Christ, to correct morbid introspection that would ground assurance in the quality of a past act of faith or in a meticulous evaluation of attainments in holiness. He would have the church rejoice in the piety of the Psalter and display a quiet confidence in a life of covenant-keeping.

All these purposes are recognized and cherished in the Reformed theological tradition. But to achieve these purposes, Mr. Shepherd would make obedience the central and embracing category for our response to God and thereby question the restrictions that the Reformed standards have put on the place and function of our good works. He urges that this can be done without danger since this obedience is not meritorious and therefore cannot become the ground of our salvation. But the very simplicity of this solution creates its danger. There is a vast and crucial difference between fleeing to Christ for salvation and serving God acceptably in new obedience. Close as the relation must be between faith and works, the distinction is central to the gospel. Mr. Shepherd does affirm a distinct function for faith, but his concept of the "dynamic" of covenantal relation effectively subordinates faith to obedience and shifts the balance in a sensitive area of great theological importance.

This distinctive aspect of his thought has been the troubling factor in these seven years of controversy. While the Board has not judged that his views are in error, the Board has come to the conviction that his views are not clearly in accord with the standards of the Seminary; for this reason it has acted within its authority to remove him from his office for the best interests of the Seminary.

A Resolution to the
Eleventh General Assembly
of the
Presbyterian Church in America

Whereas the pursuit of truth with integrity is essential to the propagation and defense of the Gospel; and

Whereas this pursuit of truth must be carried on with Christian love and sensitivity but without respect of persons or institutions; and

Whereas the attached history of the "current justification controversy" among Reformed and Presbyterian churches in America has been submitted to the theological journal of Covenant Theological Seminary by a Faculty member of the Seminary; and

Whereas the Editorial Committee of this journal (*Presbyterion*) has commended this article as a fair representation of the issues currently before the church so far as it can determine, noting that the material "must" be published, and even offering to assist financially in its publication; and

Whereas this Committee, and then by a vote of five to four with two abstentions, the Faculty of Covenant Seminary voted not to publish this article in its journal, giving as its reason that it might be offensive to another respected seminary of the Reformed and Presbyterian family in America; and

Whereas the author of this article has expressed his openness to editorial suggestions, and his willingness to have other viewpoints on this issue printed in subsequent editions of *Presbyterion* so long as they are factually true and promote the doctrinal positions of the Presbyterian Church in America; and

Whereas due to this church's relation to Covenant Theological Seminary, *Presbyterion* in some senses serves as the organ for ongoing theological discussion within the Presbyterian Church in America, and not merely the organ of Covenant Theological Seminary; and

Whereas the policies and decisions related to Covenant Theological Seminary are subject to the review and control of the Presbyterian Church in America;

Therefore the Presbyterian Church in America is respectfully requested to determine whether or not the pages of *Presbyterion* should be open to this article on the current justification controversy.

Respectfully submitted,
O. Palmer Robertson

The General Assembly of the PCA rejected the Resolution, and *The Current Justification Controversy* never appeared in *Presbyterion* or any other theological journal. It was suppressed by the Faculty of Covenant Theological Seminary. Twenty years later, it is appearing in print for the first time.

– Publisher

Index

Scripture Index

The Crisis of Our Time

HISTORIANS have christened the thirteenth century the Age of Faith and termed the eighteenth century the Age of Reason. The present age has been called many things: the Atomic Age, the Age of Inflation, the Age of the Tyrant, the Age of Aquarius; but it deserves one name more than the others: the Age of Irrationalism. Contemporary secular intellectuals are anti-intellectual. Contemporary philosophers are anti-philosophy. Contemporary theologians are anti-theology.

In past centuries, secular philosophers have generally believed that knowledge is possible to man. Consequently they expended a great deal of thought and effort trying to justify knowledge. In the twentieth century, however, the optimism of the secular philosophers all but disappeared. They despaired of knowledge.

Like their secular counterparts, the great theologians and doctors of the church taught that knowledge is possible to man. Yet the theologians of the present age also repudiated that belief. They too despaired of knowledge. This radical skepticism has penetrated our entire culture, from television to music to literature. *The Christian at the beginning of the twenty-first century is confronted with an overwhelming cultural consensus — sometimes stated explicitly but most often implicitly: Man does not and cannot know anything truly.*

What does this have to do with Christianity? Simply this: If man can know nothing truly, man can truly know nothing. We cannot know that the Bible is the Word of God, that Christ died for his people, or that Christ is alive today at the right hand of the Father. Unless knowledge is possible, Christianity is nonsensical, for it claims to be knowledge. What is at stake at the beginning of the twenty-first century is not simply a single doctrine, such as the virgin birth, or the existence of Hell, as important as those doctrines may be, but the whole of Christianity itself. If knowledge is not possible to man, it is worse than silly to argue points of doctrine – it is insane.

The irrationalism of the present age is so thoroughgoing and pervasive that even the Remnant – the segment of the professing church that remains faithful – has accepted much of it, frequently without even being aware of what it is accepting. In some religious circles this irrationalism has become synonymous with piety and humility, and those who oppose it are denounced as rationalists, as though to be logical were a sin. Our contemporary anti-theologians make a contradiction and call it a Mystery. The faithful ask for truth and are given Paradox and Antinomy. If any balk at swallowing the absurdities of the anti-theologians who teach in the seminaries or have graduated from the seminaries, they are frequently marked as heretics or schismatics who seek to act independently of God.

There is no greater threat facing the church of Christ at this moment than the irrationalism that now controls our entire culture. Totalitarianism, guilty of tens of millions of murders – including those of millions of Christians – is to be feared, but not nearly so much as the idea that we do not and cannot know the literal truth. Hedonism, the popular philosophy of

America, is not to be feared so much as the belief that logic – that "mere human logic," to use the religious irrationalists' own phrase – is futile. The attacks on truth, on knowledge, on propositional revelation, on the intellect, on words, and on logic are renewed daily. But note well: The misologists – the haters of logic – use logic to demonstrate the futility of using logic. The anti-intellectuals construct intricate intellectual arguments to prove the insufficiency of the intellect. Those who deny the competence of words to express thought use words to express their thoughts. The proponents of poetry, myth, metaphor, and analogy argue for their theories by using literal prose, whose competence – even whose possibility – they deny. The anti-theologians use the revealed Word of God to show that there can be no revealed Word of God – or that if there could, it would remain impenetrable darkness and Mystery to our finite minds.

Nonsense Has Come

Is it any wonder that the world is grasping at straws – the straws of experientialism, mysticism, and drugs? After all, if people are told that the Bible contains insoluble mysteries, then is not a flight into mysticism to be expected? On what grounds can it be condemned? Certainly not on logical grounds or Biblical grounds, if logic is futile and the Bible unknowable. Moreover, if it cannot be condemned on logical or Biblical grounds, it cannot be condemned at all. If people are going to have a religion of the mysterious, they will not adopt Christianity: They will have a genuine mystery religion. The popularity of mysticism, drugs, and religious experience is the logical consequence of the irrationalism of the present age. There can and will be no Christian reformation – and no restoration of a free society – unless and until the irrational-ism of the age is totally repudiated by Christians.

The Church Defenseless

Yet how shall they do it? The official spokesmen for Christianity have been fatally infected with irrationalism. The seminaries, which annually train thousands of men to teach millions of Christians, are the finishing schools of irrationalism, completing the job begun by the government schools and colleges. Most of the pulpits of the conservative churches (we are not speaking of the obviously apostate churches) are occupied by graduates of the anti-theological schools. These products of modern anti-theological education, when asked to give a reason for the hope that is in them, can generally respond with only the intellectual analogue of a shrug – a mumble about Mystery. They have not grasped – and therefore cannot teach those for whom they are responsible – the first truth: "And you shall know the truth." Many, in fact, explicitly contradict Christ, saying that, at best, we possess only "pointers" to the truth, or something "similar" to the truth, a mere analogy. Is the impotence of the Christian church a puzzle? Is the fascination with Pentecostalism, faith healing, Eastern Orthodoxy, and Roman Catholicism – all sensate and anti-intellectual religions – among members of Christian churches an enigma? Not when one understands the pious nonsense that is purveyed in the name of God in the religious colleges and seminaries.

The Trinity Foundation

The creators of The Trinity Foundation firmly believe that theology is too important to be left to the licensed theologians

– the graduates of the schools of theology. They have created The Trinity Foundation for the express purpose of teaching the faithful all that the Scriptures contain – not warmed over, baptized, Antichristian philosophies. Each member of the board of directors of The Trinity Foundation has signed this oath: "I believe that the Bible alone and the Bible in its entirety is the Word of God and, therefore, inerrant in the autographs. I believe that the system of truth presented in the Bible is best summarized in the *Westminster Confession of Faith.* So help me God."

The ministry of The Trinity Foundation is the presentation of the system of truth taught in Scripture as clearly and as completely as possible. We do not regard obscurity as a virtue, nor confusion as a sign of spirituality. Confusion, like all error, is sin, and teaching that confusion is all that Christians can hope for is doubly sin.

The presentation of the truth of Scripture necessarily involves the rejection of error. The Foundation has exposed and will continue to expose the irrationalism of the present age, whether its current spokesman be an existentialist philosopher or a professed Reformed theologian. We oppose anti-intellectualism, whether it be espoused by a Neo-orthodox theologian or a fundamentalist evangelist. We reject misology, whether it be on the lips of a Neo-evangelical or those of a Roman Catholic Charismatic. We repudiate agnosticism, whether it be secular or religious. To each error we bring the brilliant light of Scripture, proving all things, and holding fast to that which is true.

The Primacy of Theory

The ministry of The Trinity Foundation is not a "practical" ministry. If you are a pastor, we will not enlighten you on how to organize an ecumenical prayer meeting in your community or how to double church attendance in a year. If you are a homemaker, you will have to read elsewhere to find out how to become a total woman. If you are a businessman, we will not tell you how to develop a social conscience. The professing church is drowning in such "practical" advice.

The Trinity Foundation is unapologetically theoretical in its outlook, believing that theory without practice is dead, and that practice without theory is blind. The trouble with the professing church is not primarily in its practice, but in its theory. Churchgoers and teachers do not know, and many do not even care to know, the doctrines of Scripture. Doctrine is intellectual, and churchgoers and teachers are generally anti-intellectual. Doctrine is ivory tower philosophy, and they scorn ivory towers. The ivory tower, however, is the control tower of a civilization. It is a fundamental, theoretical mistake of the "practical" men to think that they can be merely practical, for practice is always the practice of some theory. The relationship between theory and practice is the relationship between cause and effect. If a person believes correct theory, his practice will tend to be correct. The practice of contemporary Christians is immoral because it is the practice of false theories. It is a major theoretical mistake of the "practical" men to think that they can ignore the ivory towers of the philosophers and theologians as irrelevant to their lives. Every action that "practical" men take is governed by the thinking that has occurred in some ivory tower – whether that tower be the British Museum; the Academy; a home in Basel, Switzerland; or a tent in Israel.

In Understanding Be Men

It is the first duty of the Christian to understand correct theory – correct doctrine – and thereby implement correct practice. This order – first theory, then practice – is both logical and Biblical. It is, for example, exhibited in Paul's *Epistle to the Romans,* in which he spends the first eleven chapters expounding theory and the last five discussing practice. The contemporary teachers of Christians have not only reversed the Biblical order, they have inverted the Pauline emphasis on theory and practice. The virtually complete failure of the teachers of the professing church to instruct believers in correct doctrine is the cause of the misconduct and spiritual and cultural impotence of Christians. The church's lack of power is the result of its lack of truth. The *Gospel* is the power of God, not religious experiences or personal relationships. The church has no power because it has abandoned the Gospel, the good news, for a religion of experientialism. Twentieth-first-century American churchgoers are children carried about by every wind of doctrine, not knowing what they believe, or even if they believe anything for certain.

The chief purpose of The Trinity Foundation is to counteract the irrationalism of the age and to expose the errors of the teachers of the church. Our emphasis – on the Bible as the sole source of knowledge, on the primacy of truth, on the supreme importance of correct doctrine, and on the necessity for systematic and logical thinking – is almost unique in Christendom. To the extent that the church survives – and she will survive and flourish – it will be because of her increasing acceptance of these basic ideas and their logical implications.

We believe that The Trinity Foundation is filling a vacuum in Christendom. We are saying that Christianity is intellectually defensible – that, in fact, it is the only intellectually defensible system of thought. We are saying that God has made the wisdom of this world – whether that wisdom be called science, religion, philosophy, or common sense – foolishness. We are appealing to all Christians who have not conceded defeat in the intellectual battle with the world to join us in our efforts to raise a standard to which all men of sound mind can repair.

The love of truth, of God's Word, has all but disappeared in our time. We are committed to and pray for a great instauration. But though we may not see this reformation in our lifetimes, we believe it is our duty to present the whole counsel of God, because Christ has commanded it. The results of our teaching are in God's hands, not ours. Whatever those results, his Word is never taught in vain, but always accomplishes the result that he intended it to accomplish. Professor Gordon H. Clark has stated our view well:

"There have been times in the history of God's people, for example, in the days of Jeremiah, when refreshing grace and widespread revival were not to be expected: The time was one of chastisement. If this twentieth century is of a similar nature, individual Christians here and there can find comfort and strength in a study of God's Word. But if God has decreed happier days for us, and if we may expect a world-shaking and genuine spiritual awakening, then it is the author's belief that a zeal for souls, however necessary, is not the sufficient condition. Have there not been devout saints in every age, numerous enough to carry on a revival? Twelve such persons are plenty. What distinguishes the arid ages from the period of the Reformation, when nations were moved as they had not been since Paul preached in Ephesus, Corinth, and Rome, is the latter's fullness of knowledge of God's Word. To echo an early Reformation thought, when the ploughman and the garage attendant know the Bible as well as the theologian does, and know it better than some contemporary theologians, then the desired awakening shall have already occurred."

In addition to publishing books, the Foundation publishes a monthly newsletter, *The Trinity Review*. Subscriptions to *The Review* are free to U.S. addresses; please write to the address on the order form to become a subscriber. If you would like further information or would like to join us in our work, please let us know.

The Trinity Foundation is a non-profit foundation, tax exempt under section 501 (c)(3) of the Internal Revenue Code of 1954. You can help us disseminate the Word of God through your tax-deductible contributions to the Foundation.

JOHN W. ROBBINS

Intellectual Ammunition

THE Trinity Foundation is committed to bringing every philosophical and theological thought captive to Christ. The books listed below are designed to accomplish that goal. They are written with two subordinate purposes: (1) to demolish all non-Christian claims to knowledge; and (2) to build a system of truth based upon the Bible alone.

Philosophy

Ancient Philosophy
Gordon H. Clark   Trade paperback $24.95
  This book covers the thousand years from the Pre-Socratics to Plotinus. It represents some of the early work of Dr. Clark – the work that made his academic reputation. It is an excellent college text.

Behaviorism and Christianity
Gordon H. Clark   Trade paperback $5.95
  Behaviorism is a critique of both secular and religious behaviorists. It includes chapters on John Watson, Edgar S. Singer, Jr., Gilbert Ryle, B. F. Skinner, and Donald MacKay. Clark's refutation of behaviorism and his argument for a Christian doctrine of man are unanswerable.

A Christian Philosophy of Education   Hardback $18.95
Gordon H. Clark   Trade paperback $12.95
   The first edition of this book was published in 1946. It
sparked the contemporary interest in Christian schools.
In the 1970s, Dr. Clark thoroughly revised and updated
it, and it is needed now more than ever. Its chapters include: The Need for a World-View; The Christian World-
View; The Alternative to Christian Theism; Neutrality;
Ethics; The Christian Philosophy of Education; Academic
Matters; and Kindergarten to University. Three appendices are included: The Relationship of Public Education to Christianity; A Protestant World-View; and Art
and the Gospel.

A Christian View of Men and Things   Hardback $29.95
Gordon H. Clark   Trade paperback $14.95
   No other book achieves what *A Christian View* does:
the presentation of Christianity as it applies to history,
politics, ethics, science, religion, and epistemology. Dr.
Clark's command of both worldly philosophy and Scripture is evident on every page, and the result is a breath-
taking and invigorating challenge to the wisdom of this
world.

Clark Speaks from the Grave
Gordon H. Clark   Trade paperback $3.95
   Dr. Clark chides some of his critics for their failure to
defend Christianity competently. *Clark Speaks* is a stimu-
lating and illuminating discussion of the errors of contemporary apologists.

Ecclesiastical Megalomania:
The Economic and Political Thought
of the Roman Catholic Church
John W. Robbins   Hardback $21.95
   This detailed and thorough analysis and critique of the
social teaching of the Roman Church-State is the only
such book available by a Christian economist and political philosopher. The book's conclusions reveal the Roman Church-State to be an advocate of its own brand of
faith-based fascism. *Ecclesiastical Megalomania* includes
the complete text of the *Donation of Constantine* and
Lorenzo Valla's exposé of the hoax.

Education, Christianity, and the State
J. Gresham Machen   Trade paperback $9.95
   Machen was one of the foremost educators, theologians, and defenders of Christianity in the twentieth century. The author of several scholarly books, Machen saw
clearly that if Christianity is to survive and flourish, a
system of Christian schools must be established. This collection of essays and speeches captures his thoughts on
education over nearly three decades.

Essays on Ethics and Politics
Gordon H. Clark   Trade paperback $10.95
   Dr. Clark's essays, written over the course of five de-
cades, are a major statement of Christian ethics.

Gordon H. Clark: Personal Recollections
John W. Robbins, editor   Trade paperback $6.95
   Friends of Dr. Clark have written their recollections of
the man. Contributors include family members, col-
leagues, students, and friends such as Harold Lindsell,
Carl Henry, Ronald Nash, and Anna Marie Hager.

Historiography: Secular and Religious
Gordon H. Clark   Trade paperback $13.95
   In this masterful work, Dr. Clark applies his philosophy to the writing of history, examining all the major
schools of historiography.

An Introduction to Christian Philosophy
Gordon H. Clark   Trade paperback $8.95
   In 1966 Dr. Clark delivered three lectures on philosophy at Wheaton College. In these lectures he criticizes
secular philosophy and launches a philosophical revolution in the name of Christ.

Language and Theology
Gordon H. Clark   Trade paperback $9.95
   There are two main currents in twentieth-century phi-
losophy – language philosophy and existentialism. Both
are hostile to Christianity. Dr. Clark disposes of language
philosophy in this brilliant critique of Bertrand Russell,
Ludwig Wittgenstein, Rudolf Carnap, A. J. Ayer, Langdon
Gilkey, and many others.

Logic   Hardback $16.95
Gordon H. Clark   Trade paperback $10.95
   Written as a textbook for Christian schools, *Logic* is
another unique book from Dr. Clark's pen. His presentation of the laws of thought, which must be followed if
Scripture is to be understood correctly, and which are
found in Scripture itself, is both clear and thorough. *Logic*
is an indispensable book for the thinking Christian.

Lord God of Truth, Concerning the Teacher
Gordon H. Clark and
Aurelius Augustine   Trade paperback $7.95
   This essay by Dr. Clark summarizes many of the most
telling arguments against empiricism and defends the
Biblical teaching that we know God and truth immedi-
ately. The dialogue by Augustine is a refutation of em-
pirical language philosophy.

The Philosophy of Science and Belief in God
Gordon H. Clark   Trade paperback $8.95
   In opposing the contemporary idolatry of science, Dr.
Clark analyzes three major aspects of science: the problem of motion, Newtonian science, and modern theories
of physics. His conclusion is that science, while it may be
useful, is always false; and he demonstrates its falsity in
numerous ways. Since science is always false, it can offer
no alternative to the Bible and Christianity.

Religion, Reason and Revelation
Gordon H. Clark   Trade paperback $10.95
   One of Dr. Clark's apologetical masterpieces, *Religion, Reason and Revelation* has been praised for the clarity of its thought and language. It includes these chapters: Is Christianity a Religion? Faith and Reason; Inspiration and Language; Revelation and Morality; and God and Evil. It is must reading for all serious Christians.

The Scripturalism of Gordon H. Clark
W. Gary Crampton   Trade paperback $9.95
   Dr. Crampton has written an introduction to the philosophy of Gordon H. Clark that is helpful to both beginners and advanced students of theology. This book includes a bibliography of Dr. Clark's works.

Thales to Dewey:
A History of Philosophy   Hardback $29.95
Gordon H. Clark   Trade paperback $21.95
   This is the best one-volume history of philosophy in print.

Three Types of Religious Philosophy
Gordon H. Clark   Trade paperback $6.95
   In this book on apologetics, Dr. Clark examines empiricism, rationalism, dogmatism, and contemporary irrationalism, which does not rise to the level of philosophy. He offers an answer to the question, "How can Christianity be defended before the world?"

William James and John Dewey
Gordon H. Clark   Trade paperback $8.95
   William James and John Dewey are two of the most
influential philosophers America has produced. Their
philosophies of instrumentalism and pragmatism are
hostile to Christianity, and Dr. Clark demolishes their
arguments.

Without A Prayer: Ayn Rand and the Close of Her System
John W. Robbins   Hardback $27.95
   Ayn Rand has been a best-selling author since 1957.
Without A Prayer discusses Objectivism's epistemology,
theology, ethics, and politics in detail. Appendices include
analyses of books by Leonard Peikoff and David Kelley,
as well as several essays on Christianity and philosophy.

Theology

Against the Churches: The Trinity Review 1989-1998
John W. Robbins, editor   Oversize hardback $39.95
   This is the second volume of essays from *The Trinity
Review*, covering its second ten years, 1989-1998. This
volume, like the first, is fully indexed and is very useful in
research and in the classroom. Authors include: Gordon
Clark, John Robbins, Charles Hodge, J. C. Ryle, Horatius
Bonar, and Robert L. Dabney.

Against the World: The Trinity Review 1978-1988
John W. Robbins, editor   Oversize hardback $34.95
   This is a clothbound collection of the essays published
in *The Trinity Review* from 1978 to 1988, 70 in all. It is a

valuable source of information and arguments explaining and defending Christianity.

The Atonement
Gordon H. Clark   Trade paperback $8.95

In *The Atonement,* Dr. Clark discusses the covenants, the virgin birth and incarnation, federal headship and representation, the relationship between God's sovereignty and justice, and much more. He analyzes traditional views of the atonement and criticizes them in the light of Scripture alone.

The Biblical Doctrine of Man
Gordon H. Clark   Trade paperback $6.95

Is man soul and body or soul, spirit, and body? What is the image of God? Is Adam's sin imputed to his children? Is evolution true? Are men totally depraved? What is the heart? These are some of the questions discussed and answered from Scripture in this book.

By Scripture Alone
W. Gary Crampton   Trade paperback $12.95

This is a clear and thorough explanation of the Scriptural doctrine of Scripture and a refutation of the recent Romanist attack on Scripture as the Word of God.

The Changing of the Guard
Mark W. Karlberg   Trade paperback $3.95

This essay is a critical discussion of Westminster Seminary's anti-Reformational and un-Biblical teaching on the doctrine of justification. Dr. Karlberg exposes the doctrine of justification by faith and works – not *sola fide* – taught at Westminster Seminary for the past 25 years, by Professors Norman Shepherd, Richard Gaffin, John Frame, and others.

The Church Effeminate
John W. Robbins, editor   Hardback $29.95
    This is a collection of 39 essays by the best theologians of the church on the doctrine of the church: Martin Luther, John Calvin, Benjamin Warfield, Gordon Clark, J. C. Ryle, and many more. The essays cover the structure, function, and purpose of the church.

The Clark-Van Til Controversy
Herman Hoeksema   Trade paperback $7.95
    This collection of essays by the founder of the Protestant Reformed Churches – essays written at the time of the Clark-Van Til controversy in the 1940s – is one of the best commentaries on those events in print.

A Companion to The Current Justification Controversy
John W. Robbins   Trade paperback $9.95
    This book includes documentary source material not available in *The Current Justification Controversy*, and an essay tracing the origins and continuation of this controversy throughout American Presbyterian churches.

Cornelius Van Til: The Man and The Myth
John W. Robbins   Trade paperback $2.45
    The actual teachings of this eminent Philadelphia theologian have been obscured by the myths that surround

him. This book penetrates those myths and criticizes Van Til's surprisingly unorthodox views of God and the Bible.

The Current Justification Controversy

O. Palmer Robertson   Trade paperback $9.95

From 1975 to 1982 a controversy over justification raged within Westminster Theological Seminary and the Philadelphia Presbytery of the Orthodox Presbyterian Church. As a member of the faculties of both Westminster and Covenant Seminaries during this period, O. Palmer Robertson was an important participant in this controversy. This is his account of the controversy, vital background for understanding the defection from the Gospel that is now widespread in Presbyterian churches.

The Everlasting Righteousness

Horatius Bonar   Trade paperback $8.95

Originally published in 1874, the language of Bonar's masterpiece on justification by faith alone has been updated and Americanized for easy reading and clear understanding. This is one of the best books ever written on justification.

Faith and Saving Faith

Gordon H. Clark   Trade paperback $6.95

The views of the Roman Catholic Church, John Calvin, Thomas Manton, John Owen, Charles Hodge, and B. B. Warfield are discussed in this book. Is the object of faith a person or a proposition? Is faith more than belief? Is belief thinking with assent, as Augustine said? In a world

chaotic with differing views of faith, Dr. Clark clearly
explains the Biblical view of faith and saving faith.

God and Evil: The Problem Solved
Gordon H. Clark   Trade paperback $4.95
  This volume is Chapter 5 of *Religion, Reason and Revelation,* in which Dr. Clark presents his solution to the
  problem of evil.

God-Breathed: The Divine Inspiration of the Bible
Louis Gaussen   Trade paperback $16.95
  Gaussen, a nineteenth-century Swiss Reformed pastor,
  comments on hundreds of passages in which the Bible
  claims to be the Word of God. This is a massive defense
  of the doctrine of the plenary and verbal inspiration of
  Scripture.

God's Hammer: The Bible and Its Critics
Gordon H. Clark   Trade paperback $10.95
  The starting point of Christianity, the doctrine on which
  all other doctrines depend, is "The Bible alone, and the
  Bible in its entirety, is the Word of God written, and, therefore, inerrant in the autographs." Over the centuries the
  opponents of Christianity, with Satanic shrewdness, have
  concentrated their attacks on the truthfulness and com-
  pleteness of the Bible. In the twentieth century the attack
  was not so much in the fields of history and archaeology
  as in philosophy. Dr. Clark's brilliant defense of the complete truthfulness of the Bible is captured in this collection of eleven major essays.

The Holy Spirit
Gordon H. Clark   Trade paperback $8.95
   This discussion of the third person of the Trinity is
both concise and exact. Dr. Clark includes chapters on
the work of the Spirit, sanctification, and Pentecostalism.
This book is part of his multi-volume systematic theology that began appearing in print in 1985.

The Incarnation
Gordon H. Clark   Trade paperback $8.95
   Who is Christ? The attack on the doctrine of the
Incarnation in the nineteenth and twentieth centuries
was vigorous, but the orthodox response was lame. Dr.
Clark reconstructs the doctrine of the Incarnation,
building and improving upon the Chalcedonian
definition.

The Johannine Logos
Gordon H. Clark   Trade paperback $5.95
   Dr. Clark analyzes the relationship between Christ, who
is the truth, and the Bible. He explains why John used the
same word to refer to both Christ and his teaching. Chapters deal with the Prologue to John's Gospel; *Logos* and
Rheemata; Truth; and Saving Faith.

Justification by Faith Alone
Charles Hodge   Trade paperback $10.95
   Charles Hodge of Princeton Seminary was the best
American theologian of the nineteenth century. Here,
for the first time, are his two major essays on justification

in one volume. This book is essential in defending the faith.

Karl Barth's Theological Method
Gordon H. Clark   Trade paperback $18.95
   Karl Barth's Theological Method is perhaps the best critique of the Neo-orthodox theologian Karl Barth ever written. Dr. Clark discusses Barth's view of revelation, language, and Scripture, focusing on his method of writing theology, rather than presenting a comprehensive analysis of the details of Barth's theology.

Logical Criticisms of Textual Criticism
Gordon H. Clark   Trade paperback $3.25
   Dr. Clark's acute mind enables him to demonstrate the inconsistencies, assumptions, and flights of fancy that characterize the science of New Testament criticism.

New Testament Greek for Beginners
J. Gresham Machen   Hardback $13.95
   Long a standard text, *New Testament Greek for Beginners* is extremely helpful in the study of the New Testament in the original Greek. It may profitably be used by high school, college, and seminary students, either in a classroom setting or in self-study. Machen was Professor of New Testament Literature and Exegesis at Princeton Theological Seminary and the founder of Westminster Theological Seminary and the Orthodox Presbyterian Church.

Predestination

Gordon H. Clark   Trade paperback $10.95

Dr. Clark thoroughly discusses one of the most controversial and pervasive doctrines of the Bible: that God is, quite literally, Almighty. Free will, the origin of evil, God's omniscience, creation, and the new birth are all presented within a Scriptural framework. The objections of those who do not believe in Almighty God are considered and refuted. This edition also contains the text of the booklet, *Predestination in the Old Testament.*

Sanctification

Gordon H. Clark   Trade paperback $8.95

In this book, which is part of Dr. Clark's multi-volume systematic theology, he discusses historical theories of sanctification, the sacraments, and the Biblical doctrine of sanctification.

Study Guide to the Westminster Confession

W. Gary Crampton   Oversize paperback $10.95

This *Study Guide* may be used by individuals or classes. It contains a paragraph-by-paragraph summary of the *Westminster Confession,* and questions for the student to answer. Space for answers is provided. The *Guide* will be most beneficial when used in conjunction with Dr. Clark's *What Do Presbyterians Believe?*

A Theology of the Holy Spirit

Frederick Dale Bruner   Trade paperback, $16.95

First published in 1970, this book has been hailed by reviewers as "thorough," "fair," "comprehensive," "devastating," "the most significant book on the Holy Spirit," and "scholarly." Gordon Clark described this book in his own book *The Holy Spirit* as "a masterly and exceedingly well researched exposition of Pentecostalism. The documentation is superb, as is also his penetrating analysis of their non-scriptural and sometimes contradictory conclusions." Unfortunately, the book is marred by the author's sacramentarianism.

The Trinity
Gordon H. Clark   Trade paperback $8.95
   Apart from the doctrine of Scripture, no teaching of the Bible is more fundamental than the doctrine of God. Dr. Clark's defense of the orthodox doctrine of the Trinity is a principal portion of his systematic theology. There are chapters on the Deity of Christ; Augustine; the Incomprehensibility of God; Bavinck and Van Til; and the Holy Spirit; among others.

What Calvin Says
W. Gary Crampton   Trade paperback $10.95
   This is a clear, readable, and thorough introduction to the theology of John Calvin.

What Do Presbyterians Believe?
Gordon H. Clark   Trade paperback $10.95
   This classic is the best commentary on the *Westminster Confession of Faith* ever written.

Clark's Commentaries
on the New Testament

Colossians	Trade paperback	$6.95
Ephesians	Trade paperback	$8.95
First Corinthians	Trade paperback	$10.95
First John	Trade paperback	$10.95
First and Second Thessalonians	Trade paperback	$5.95
New Heavens, New Earth		
(*First* and *Second Peter*)	Trade paperback	$10.95
The Pastoral Epistles	Hardback	$29.95
(*1* and *2 Timothy* and *Titus*)	Trade paperback	$14.95
Philippians	Trade paperback	$9.95

All of Clark's commentaries are expository, not technical, and are written for the Christian layman. His purpose is to explain the text clearly and accurately so that the Word of God will be thoroughly known by every Christian.

The Trinity Library

We will send you one copy of each of the 59 books listed above for $500 (retail value $800), postpaid to any address in the U.S. You may also order the books you want individually on the order form on the next page. Because some of the books are in short supply, we must reserve the right to substitute others of equal or greater value in The Trinity Library. This special offer expires October 31, 2006.

Order Form

NAME _____

ADDRESS _____

_____

TELEPHONE _____

E-MAIL _____

Please:

❑ add my name to the mailing list for *The Trinity Review.*
I understand that there is no charge for single copies of
The Review sent to a U. S. address.

❑ accept my tax deductible contribution of $ _____ .

❑ send me _____ copies of *A Companion to The Current
Justification Controversy.* I enclose as payment U.S.
$ _____.

❑ send me the Trinity Library of 59 books. I enclose
U.S. $500 as full payment.

❑ send me the following books. I enclose full payment in
the amount of U.S. $ _____ for them.

_____

_____

_____

_____

The Trinity Foundation
Post Office Box 68
Unicoi, Tennessee 37692
Website: http://www.trinityfoundation.org/
United States of America

Shipping: Please add $6.00 for the first book, and 50 cents
for each additional book. For foreign orders, please add $1.00
for each additional book.